WOMAN OF EMPIRE

A Biography of

Mary Ann Pelly

≈

SARAH LAWLEY

Published by Sarah Lawley

ISBN 978-1-78222-608-6

Book design, layout and production management by Into Print
www.intoprint.net
+44 (0)1604 832149

Acknowledgements

The following people have given me help and advice:

Thomas Lawley, George Pelly, Jessamy Reynolds, Jonathan Lawley, Jane Claydon

CONTENTS

Acknowledgements   3

CHAPTER 1 7
   October 1992 10
   Pictures from Rhona's Album 13

CHAPTER 2: *Mary Ann* 17

CHAPTER 3: *My Mother's Story* 21

CHAPTER 4: *India* 41
   Photos of life in India and Afghanistan ... 59

CHAPTER 5: *Coming Home* 64
   Bernard 71
   Move to Salisbury 71
   The Neighbours 73
   Growing Up 74
   Robin 75

CHAPTER 6: *Mary Ann and Cars* 77

CHAPTER 7: *The Green, 1955-70s* 82

CHAPTER 8: 89

CHAPTER 9: *MA's Friends* 94
   Chris Royle 94
   Fat D 96
   Babs 97
   Others 98

Photographs: Peshawar, 1930s 100
Appendix 1: Letter of condolence 107
Appendix 2: Harry's letters from the Front ... 108
Appendix 3: Collected poems 114

Chapter 1

Born 3rd June, 1901
Died 14th November, 1992

1901-13	Galashiels
1913-19	Edinburgh, Education; St Leonards, St Georges, St Margarets
1920-23	Cambridge MA History/Economics
1923-24	Continent/Canada
1924-30	South Africa
1930-34	New Zealand
1934-35	Scotland/Continent
1935-47	India, N W Frontier, Afghanistan.

(1939 married HPN Pelly Scotland)

1945 widowed

1947	Scotland returned England.
1947-92	Devon and Salisbury

1st October 1992

New Hall, Annexe (old workhouse), Odstock Hospital, Salisbury, Wilts.

Mary Ann

"Ah Sarah! Let me introduce you to my daughter, Sarah."

The two old ladies were sitting together looking very cheerful. My mother smartly dressed in a blouse and skirt, a little island of normality in an ocean of misery.

"What's your name again?" Mary Ann asked her friend.

"I'm Valery. Hello Sarah! Your mother and I have been setting up 'An Escape Committee'!"

"I don't blame you, this is the most dreadful place," said I.

WOMEN SURGICAL could only be described as Bedlam. Old women with wild white hair lay propped up, some screaming loudly, others, soundlessly raging at the iniquities of the staff, ranged in beds along the walls. The overall pervasive scent was urine.

"Mary Ann was telling me about her leg; she says she smashed herself up in a car," said Valery, a kindred spirit, elderly craggy-featured and dressed in brown; she was about to be let out.

Mary Ann chipped in, "That's why I have to wear these football boots!" She raised her foot in a boot laced up to the knee.

"Well the last crash was ten years ago, Mum! And there were many before that!" I interjected. Actually, it was the sixth car crash that I could remember; I was born when she was 40, so how many more before I was born?

My mother looked shamefaced but quite gleeful.

I was encouraged by the fact that she was enjoying shocking her new-found friend. I egged her on.

"You remember, only a few years ago you backed into someone's lawnmower when you were turning in their drive! But I suppose it could not really be counted as a car crash, just an argument."

"Nonsense!"

"You remember after playing bridge at the Bartholomew's!"

"Oh yes! That WAS awful. I paid him out a cheque immediately and he promised not to tell, but when I had gone he ran straight across the road and told them. How they laughed."

Mary Ann looked even more roguish. "What a rotter! I had a bit of damage too! Imagine leaving your lawnmower in your drive!"

Valery reassessed my mother. They had been having a long, erudite discussions on Shakespeare the day before. Valery had some theory that the Bard's works had some mathematical link, which my mother rudely ridiculed to me later.

That was how I remember her, full of confidence, fun and joy.

She had fallen in the hallway in her cottage. Her friendly cleaner, Mrs Feltham – 'F' – the light of her life, had turned the mat in the hall around and she had tripped up on it. Her built-up shoe had caught on it and she had broken her hip; but it was mending and all was well.

Two weeks later, Valery had escaped and my mother was still there.

"Would you like some fresh air? It's a nice afternoon, the rain has stopped and the sun might be coming out."

"Yes, I'd love to get out of this mad-house!"

The wheelchair skewed and tipped as I manhandled it with ease onto a pavement outside the hospital; I pushed it along past bright cotoneaster berries hung with raindrops which showered down on the crouching bundle of my mother. The old lady did not notice the drips but she was transfixed by the radiance of some nerines, bright purple in the autumn light. Mary Ann chirped and squinted at the bright colours, thoroughly enjoying a trip out. She had been there for a month: it was the old workhouse, a huge ward full of the very poor and ill old women. She was better now but knew she would not be going home again. Although her nerines would be out at home, beside the patio wall where they had been for years, the patch growing bigger every year until they started to come up between the paving stones she said nothing, there was no point in mentioning them.

We could be recognised as mother and daughter, both had big noses, one thin and hooked the other thicker and smaller. The set of eyes was the same, but the older woman's glinted, sharp and twinkly, whilst the other was more astute and calculating. The little face of the old lady was alight with interest and excitement and a huge smile transformed her into her old self again.

"What's that beautiful tree? Isn't it lovely!" she said, pointing to a small Japanese Acer in the garden of a bungalow that bordered the hospital.

"It's Japanese, an ornamental tree, they don't harbour any native life," said I rather tartly.

"Why does everything have to harbour native life? Can't I like things just because they are beautiful?"

The sedate bungalows and neatly trimmed lawns were far from beautiful, but the tree stood out like a small orange and gold flame, a symbol of hope in the dreary, mediocre surroundings.

"Yes, you're right; its lovely isn't it! You've always surrounded yourself with beautiful things," I sounded ingratiating again.

"Rubbish, I own nothing of value, but I like things to be pretty and cheerful."

This was true: her house always looked well cared for with shining silver and nice pictures on the walls. She was always smartly dressed and while she thought of herself as ugly – and certainly was a bit – her appeal lay in her expression and lively interest in everything.

"Shall we go back to prison now? Are you tired?" I asked.

"Yes, do. You must be tired of pushing this enormous chair". (Always worrying about others!)

"No, I'm not tired – you weigh nothing. Let's go on to the end and see what's happening to the new road. Just say if you're cold, at least prison is warm!"

There was silence for a time and then the old lady said, "Did I ever tell you about the time I was in prison in Russia?" I'd heard the story many times before and had never listened, there were so many 'did I ever tell you's'.

"When I had just come down from Cambridge I had a boyfriend who was working on The Times, and he and some other friends, also just down from

Cambridge, had the chance to go to Russia just after the Revolution. The new Revolutionaries wanted the West to know how wonderful it all was. We went by ship to Leningrad, the name has changed now, but we went to the palaces and to the places they wanted us to see. Then we decided on our own to go to the docks to see their ships. I can't remember why, but we were all thrown into prison for the night. It was terribly cold and dank and terrifying and in the morning they let us out. We had to leave immediately afterwards. They realised too late that we had been invited and were there to give them some good publicity. Ha Ha"

"When was that exactly?"

"Oh, I can't remember. Just after I came down from Cambridge in about 1923."

October 1992

I had driven down to the hospital to see my mother, aged ninety-two, who had broken her hip; it had been operated on and had mended well. But the nurse had told her to walk alone to the toilet in her slippers, not her built-up shoes. She had fallen and broken her other good leg. This really was disaster. Thankfully for all concerned, she had not been able to drive for the last ten years, but although that last car crash had finished off her passenger, Babs, it had not finished her off. Her hip femur was left out of its socket but did not hurt she said and she had hobbled around for eleven years with her leg getting shorter and shorter. However, she still led a very full life: she lived alone, tended her garden, read prodigiously, watched her telly, terrorised her neighbours and daughter in law, played bridge, filled the house with people and had dozens of parties.

But that was all over now and she knew it.

When I see old ladies in their motorised wheelchairs, slowly motoring along the pavement, I feel so envious. They have escaped Bedlam, Woman's Surgical and they can go out into the sun or rain whenever they want. I don't think, 'You poor old thing!' rather I think, 'If only it was Mum, she'd be so happy to be out and free!' She would have her social life and her Bridge Four, with all its laughter, sherry and cigarettes.

We looked at the new road, there were new lights and lines and one-way systems, zebras, slows, crossing points, flashing bollards.

"I don't recognise it at all," she grumbled mystified.

"Oh Mum. Come on! Just down there you hit that bollard, you remember!"

The old lady tried to turn her whole body around and look up at me, her smile broadening.

"I never hit a bull! What are you talking about? But I do remember once in

India killing a cow! It was awful! The people gathered around and wailed and cried and I got into terrible trouble and had to pay for it with an offering in the temple!"

"It was way before the war and we had been climbing and I was very tired. I was driving quite slowly and it just came out at me."

Mary Ann Pelly shut her eyes very tightly and her memory swooped back nearly sixty years to 1934.

"There was a funny little chap called Jim. He wrote a book about our climb and I was in the book. We went on a proper mountain about 18,000 ft. He got a couple of Sherpa porters don't ask me where he got them from, and we went up the Kolahoi valley, but further. We had a really rather good time, quite a lot of fun, I never liked him much but this time we got up quite high and were climbing well and were above the snow line. We had to sleep in snow caves which the porters dug out for us. Have you seen the photos? I was OK but he got the most raging toothache and had to come down and so we never climbed it. And then on the way back I killed a cow!"

The times all get muddled up and it's only the incidents that stay for ever; it does not really matter when. They are like bubbles in your brain; they float down and remind you of another life.

"Were you living on a houseboat with Chris Royle and her sister Kit at the time, surely?"

"Yes, you're right."

"Didn't people disapprove of you going off alone into Afghanistan with a man? And, what about Eddie Fluett?"

"Nonsense they were both queer, he was a District Commissioner everyone knew. I was quite safe."

"So you must have killed the cow in Kashmir!"

"Yes it must have been in India that I killed the cow! Actually it was only a very young one and it bounded out and HIT me!"

"Liar!"

"Yes, I hadn't a hope. It just ran into the road."

I can imagine her memories of Peshawar: hunting on the pony Grenadine in the early morning; seeing the sun rise over the Himalayas; jumping over the banks and ditches after the jackals. She was always happy on a horse.

Mary Ann loved Peshawar. She did a lot of climbing and when the school closed for the summer she took to the Himalayas. She climbed with Eddie Fluett.

I remember her telling me. "It was a little way into Tibet, he was great fun to climb with and I suppose in a way he was completely sexless. There was never any question of anything going on; we were so tired at the end of the day. He was a very good linguist and as we went up the valley the language changed. You see we started with Kashmiri then a little more Chinese or Tibetan and he was always able to speak to the local porters. He was so nice and gentle and we went up as far as we could go. The only nasty thing was that he had a gun with him and his idea was that he would shoot for the pot the *oryx*, the mountain goat, but they looked so happy browsing on the hillside that in the end we did not want to disturb them. Fluett gave us that picture of the Peshawar Vale Hunt as a wedding present, I never saw him after the war or after I left Peshawar."

"Shall we go back now? I've brought you a little red Album which was your mother's. I thought we could go through it together."

"Oh Darling, how lovely. I'd love to have another look at it!"

"Look Mum! You can see the roof of River Vale – you know that nice home we want you to go to. "

"What a bloody awful idea going to live in that place!! I couldn't bear to go into that Home. A little room like a rabbit hutch. And No Smoking! But I would never be able to cope on my own at the cottage, even with a living-in help. I would have to get rid of Mrs. Feltham, and I can't possibly do that, and I can't afford it anyway. The little I have to leave would all be drained away. Drained away like I would like my life to be, full of morphine and sail away on the gentle clouds of peace.

But thinking of death fills me with terror though. What is out there? Always I have planned what was going to happen. I have always been the author of my life. I took big decisions even as a child.

When I think of my penury now and how rich we were then and why was I cut out of their Wills, the injustice of it, real injustice!"

She caught a cold that day in the rain and wind and had already decided to starve herself, I could tell. She would take a huge bite of delicious food, then remember to stop eating, one could see what she was up to! Her cold turned to pneumonia and the hospital telephoned me in London asked me if she should go onto anti-biotics and as she was so miserable especially since she knew she could not return home, I said no.

I bitterly regret it, but it was as much her choice as mine, the trouble is there was so much still to ask her.

Birklands Finishing School (to remove Scotch accent).

Birklands Ladies Cricket Team.

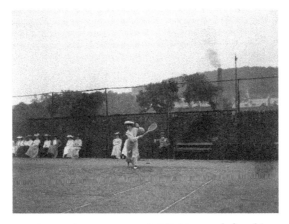

Rhona playing tennis. (Mill chimney behind.)

Harry in the garden at Eastmount (having planted seeds).

Children in Eastmount garden
(playing with Ovens's next door; B top, M third).

On the beach at Bamburgh.

The Old School House, Bamburgh.

Well brought up child.

Veronica Rutherford

My Grandmother, Veronica Rutherford, aka Rhona

Chapter 2

MARY ANN

THIS WILL I hope, paint a picture of Mary Ann for those who have never met her. I want to write down all I remember about my mother and I shall start with her baby book which had an exciting career of its own. It was given to my grandmother before she went to finishing school in St Albans. It's got "Writing Album" gold embossed on the front, the pages are different colours like an autograph book. The name Veronica Rutherford, Galashiels is on the flyleaf. It was her Autograph/ later to become baby book/ and is dated 15th January 1894. Galashiels.

The first entries date from April 7th /94 an exquisite painting from HM Royle.

There are poems and quotes, but the book became a photograph album of her nearest and dearest.

("Birklands was where they were sent to get rid of their scotch accents" Mary Ann told me contemptuously) Birklands it was near St Albans. It was later a boarding school for girls and Mary Ann's younger cousin Jane went there.

Rhona evidently got the book before going there. Then the next entry is in Harry Sanderson's writing dated 15th August, 1894. "The quality of mercy is not strained....from the Merchant of Venice

He knew her character by then and it is quite apt perhaps, he married her. There are lots of photos of Harry in the RFA Royal Field Artillery (probably the most recently entered).

The next entry is by Laura M Smith dated July 23rd and is even more apt.

"Be strong and very courageous, act for the best, hope for the best and take what comes" by Channing.

Rhona had a very sad life losing Harry in the War in 1917. Not getting on with her eldest daughter must have been very difficult too

The Autograph entries continue interspaced with photographs and it is difficult to know the dates but one picture shows the Birklands Ladies cricket team all in boaters, bow ties long wide skirts with white blouses and very tight belts. Two tired looking gentlemen must be the team coaches.

There are no wedding photographs a proper album for that no doubt once existed.

The tennis court shows Rhona playing tennis with the tall chimney in the background. Galashiels was a centre for the manufacture of tweed. From within the multi-coloured paged Writing Album emerge the first photographs of Merion Veronica Sanderson, my mother, who changed her name to 'Mary Ann' as she could not bear Merion which is Marion with an 'e'. There are many different spellings, I ask the reader's forbearance with the variants and mutations of her name! As happens in every family being the firstborn there are dozens of snaps: in this case mostly of enormous white bonnets and cascades of lace in giant perambulators with wheels similar to that of a penny farthing. Rhona holds up her adorable baby Merion, Mother and baby then a photo of sheepish looking Father holding a handful of telegrams. House in the background tells a story, a sunny day in June, (Merion was born on third June 1901) and the blinds are pulled down to stop the sun.

There is a photograph of all six sons, two of whom ran the mill, one was a solicitor, one a judge and one a stage door Johnny. There are snaps of Merion holding a man's hand, and I feel it must be the stage door Johnny! He got some girl into trouble called Myrtle and my mother remembers accompanying her mother to visit Myrtle and her family when they moved to Edinburgh. He was employed as an Articled Clerk for a Rutherford cousin and was given the sack for idleness, so the story goes. Robert went to South Africa he was a year younger than Harry and went to Rhodesia and Heather Valentine his granddaughter became a best friend of (me) Sarah Lawley, Harry's granddaughter!

These photos show that life for the little Sandersons was fun in the days before the First World War. Their cousins Ovens' lived next door and they climbed over the wall at the top of the garden where it was very low and played with the girls and boys. Boys doing handstands and Merion with no socks on just sandals. Betty was 3 years younger and had long-lashed dark-blue eyes whereas at the age of 10 Marian is already wearing glasses which she wore for the rest of her life.

Rhona had always been a keen tennis player and walked to the tennis court to play. Her mother who lived in Hoebridge, Melrose (a mansion) also pictured complained bitterly that she would wear out her shoes walking to the tennis club. (She was terribly mean). There is a picture of Rhona playing in a woman's singles match. Mary Ann also took up tennis and played at Wimbledon she served two aces she says and never got another point against Leglant and no doubt was taught and encouraged by her mother. (She says her mother was jealous of her which I am sure was true). Rhona was the first woman in the borders to own her own car. She drove a De Dion Bouton. One day she was out with the children and drove into a quarry and they all had to walk home! After the De Dion Bouton, they had a Ford then an Armstrong Sidley which was very grand and actually had a roof! This was only just before the advent of powered flight. Mary Ann recalls "When I was about eight I saw the first Air Race from London to Edinburgh, the whistle whistled and everybody came out of the Mill to watch and we saw these two tiny little black dots coming down the Gala Valley.! This was the first race about 1909.

There are lots of holiday photos on the beach at Bamburgh. Once again Mary Ann told, 'when we went to Bamburgh we went by train and were met by a wagonette. My father did not come with us. He may have come for weekends'. What a happy childhood. In her old age she talked about it a lot. Those memories of over 85 years ago when she was a little girl in Galashiels and their summer holidays at Bamburgh.

By any standards here was a rich family and since Mary Ann was the only child to have any descendants it is surprising that she was so poor. She always said that she had nothing. As children my brother and I thought it was true. She was always saying how broke she was.

"I have had a horrid letter from the Bank!"

"What did it say?"

"I don't know, I haven't dared open it! "

She said, "But you always had everything, didn't you? You never felt deprived!"

We didn't, we were both, my brother George and I thoroughly spoilt, we could do anything we wanted, she never said No! Although we knew we were poor.

My uncle Kenneth once said "Marion was very difficult, she and Mother never got on", he mentioned once that my mother had been given her share of her father's money before she had gone to South Africa. I think this was so and she bought her house in Salisbury with it. She told me that the rest of the money was badly invested and left in a trust for us the children. Betty and Kenneth had had their share in 1949 when Rhona died and had reinvested it so that is why they were very well off.

So because she was deemed improvident she was left out of the Will of her mother and her aunt Minnie. She never stopped making a fuss. "The injustice of it", she would cry, "I can't bear injustice". It evidently struck home because Kenneth left her everything, and yet he was far closer to Betty. Mary Ann was amazed at the date of the Will which had been signed 11 years earlier at a time when she said was not getting on with Kenneth. Whereas in their last few years they got on very well and were very fond of each other. Betty I think must have had the lion's share of Rhona's money. She was very astute and her money grew and grew. Mary Ann had always dismissed Kenneth as a poor thing, Mother's darling.

Tweed Mill went bankrupt after the 1929 recession. Harry might well have taken it on had he lived. Mary Ann said in later years she should have stayed in Scotland and run it instead of going off to South Africa. Family pressures evidently had their effect on her in those days, and the presence of her mother was too much to bear. Rhona had been an indomitable woman. The younger children, Betty and Kenneth adored her, but her elder daughter and she were chalk and cheese.

"My mother always hated me, she said "I hope your daughter treats you like you treat me!" Isn't that a horrible thing to say?"

So we close the Writing Album which is also full of photographs of Harry with his Regiment and the huge guns, it must have been Rhona's most precious possession. Yet it has a strange history.

Chapter 3

MY MOTHER'S STORY

THIS IS MY mother's story. I never knew my father, Henry Patrick Neville Pelly who was killed in the war, in a plane crash in February, 1945.

She was born in 1901and christened Merian Veronica Sanderson, but hated it and changed it to Marion then to Mary Ann when she caught the boat to South Africa in 1924 aged 23. Aka Mary Ann and MA.

I only knew her when she was a poor widow with two children, teaching for a living. I was born when she was forty and my brother three years later. She always worried about money, although she spent very freely. She plied me with new clothes and was very generous. She got horrid letters from the bank, sometimes she said she didn't dare open them! She had a permanent overdraft of £500 and was paid very well by the Salisbury College of Further Education, known as the 'Tech' where she taught English and History. The Bank Manager she counted as a friend and often when she went in to National and Grindlays which she called NatWest in those days, she would take sweets to the cashiers for their children, because she had taught them English at the Commerce Department. Even so, as a child I worried about her and us as a family. She seemed so old and so poor! But her childhood before the First World War up to the age of 23 had been very happy and indeed in her old age she often said she wanted to write about it. Considering her background of luxury and privilege, one might say that she had fallen on hard times, she hadn't fallen she had jumped!

Her family were lawyers and manufacturers. They came from the Borders of Scotland. The Sandersons were probably descended from shepherds who became weavers and who during the Industrial Revolution came south from the Highlands and started woollen mills on the Gala River where the rapids enter the Tweed. In 1792 the population of Galashiels was 581 and grew to 50,000 with a total of 28 working watermills by 1900. The mill owners built themselves huge mansions out of town. The Sanderson family was no exception, they owned one of the largest and richest mills. It was the first to change from water to coal power and they were the first to produce brightly coloured tartans. Robert Sanderson was Deacon of the Manufacturers Corporation in 1872. They built The Sanderson Fever Hospital which was later demolished and Kingsknowes Retirement Village has been erected on the site. Robert and his brother William never married but a younger brother James inherited it and built Abbots Mill and Robert, his son my mother's grandfather took over and he built Tweed Mill. He had eight sons and a daughter and Harry, Mary Ann's father was the fifth son. The woollen mill owners had grown rich quite quickly, the advent of the railway helped enormously. There were lots of railway lines in the borders in the mid 1800's, transport by rail was very popular, a letter dated 1866 complains about the trains so nothing has changed! The mill owners paid no taxes. Wages were very low and Galashiels became the centre of the tweed and woollen industry.

Marion a very well brought up child, she knew those long forgotten baronial mansions and Italianate villas which have long since been pulled down. She went to tea-dances in their huge conservatories with palm trees in them. Harry, her father was born at Knowepark, (demolished 1995) Windyknow Road, Galashiels and went to Edinburgh Academy as all the rest of his brothers had done. His father, the son of a self-made man was not well educated. As happens with so many successful industrialists, who had spent the best parts of their lives with noisy machinery, his offspring let him down. He worked terribly hard so that his family could live in luxury. When the time came for the children to take on the mantle of the 'trade' only the eldest, Arthur followed in his father's coal-dust footsteps. The other high-minded sons eschewed the factory, with its steam and whistles, blanket of coal dust everywhere and opted to become barristers, solicitors, architects and explorers. Their parents bequeathed money and property to build hospitals and retirement homes.

I hear my mother's voice, 'They were generous to worthy causes, but I was not one of them!'

Here are six of the eight Sanderson sons in 1890:

Arthur and John seated. Standing from left: Harry, Kenneth, Robert, Spencer (Alex and Frank missing).

(There is a family resemblance between Robert and Heather Valentine in Zimbabwe)

At the turn of the century Knowepark had a lift, installed for an old aunt. But most of the male children set off for adventure in the Empire. Spencer to Canada, Frank to Egypt, Robert (junior) to South Africa. Robert died of leprosy in Southern Rhodesia having been a pioneer. Mary Ann will have been to stay with him and his wife in 1920's.

Arthur and later Harry ran the mill, and in 1899 Harry married Rhona – (Veronica) Rutherford. Rhona was born in 1878 to Alexander and Marion Rutherford (she was 7 years younger than Harry). Alexander Rutherford was a solicitor in Melrose and he fathered his first child aged 40! They knew Sir Walter Scott who would set his watch by the grandfather clock (ours) in the Melrose Office every morning.

Rhona was second youngest of ten children, six boys and four girls. Alexander's brother was David Rutherford who went to New Zealand. His son Ernest was later to return to Cambridge as a physicist to split the atom and became the famous Sir Ernest Rutherford. My mother was his great niece and knew him well when she was at Cambridge. The old man, Alexander had one of the first cars in the Borders. He built a garage but could not reverse, so he built a turntable and the car was turned round for him each time. Rhona was the first woman to drive in Galashiels and Mary Ann remembers as a child them all going for a drive with Rhona who could not reverse either and they all had to walk home.

In the early 1900's Mary Ann had a very happy childhood. She was the eldest and most photographed baby in her family. In that luxurious album of coloured pages there are about 3 pictures of Betty and one of Kenneth and all the rest of Mary Anne (and of course her father in the Great War). She had been thoroughly spoilt by all her many uncles and aunts. Her favourite aunt was her mother's younger sister, Kitty, who lived in London and there is a family joke in which Mary Anne says,

'Aunty Kitty's come down from London and she hasn't brought me nuffink, nuffink nuffink at all!'

She was definitely demanding! Kitty was always very generous to her and in later life made up for that particular lapse a hundred-fold.

Mary Ann was always saying what an idyllic childhood she had had in those wonderful years before 1914. Photographs show the children playing with their cousins doing cartwheels and handstands, in white pinafores. But Rhona had found her first born daughter an extremely difficult child. More of that later.

They were always indulged, and there is a tale that at a birthday party, during a game of hide and seek, the children hid in the attic where the honey-combs had been laid down and they trod honey all over the house! At home in Galashiels before the Great War the Sanderson's lived at 'Eastmount' a large house on the edge of a hill with a lovely garden and lots of interesting flowers. Harry was planning to join Edinburgh University as a botanist when the War started. He had never had to worry about money or his future. As a young man he grew interested in botany and his family encouraged him, and he went to the Himalayas collecting primulas. He went with a friend and together they became the world experts on primulas. They even wrote a book about them. He once grew a white

Meconopsis (Himalayan blue poppy) and botanists from all over the country came to see it. He did not enjoy running the mill with Arthur when his father, Robert died.

Betty aged 5 with Marion aged 8 and Daddy, Harry at Eastmount.

Harry adored his family and I can imagine loved to commune with and chaff his daughters, the thin clever Marion and the sturdy, more amenable Betty. Marion had been her father's favourite, or so she thought, as he was certainly her favourite parent and together they had climbed the hills surrounding Galashiels and she told how she left the brace for her teeth on a rabbit scrape and the next day they returned and found it! Her abiding passion for climbing was fostered by her father who also loved the mountains. Although she had a governess and a nurse to look after her, she always felt she needed more, like so many bright children, she was demanding. Harry felt an affinity with his daughter who was inhibited by the Victorian conformities and principals of living in the early 1900's. Although in the past he had tried to help run the family manufacturing business, he had escaped the boredom of the Mill to make forays into the Far East, as well as the Himalayas, where a cousin had built lighthouses around the coast of China. She would later follow his example and travel to that part of the world.

Harry's family the Sanderson's and his wife's family the Rutherford's were very much part of the closely related fabric of the Gala' community. The Sanderson's had nine children and the Rutherford's eleven. So Mary Ann had many doting uncles and aunts around to spoil her.

Harry had married Veronica Rutherford in 1898; his brother John had left the Mill to go into politics so he felt obliged to help out. Until then he had been free to travel and pursue his interests. But marriage brought him home to Gala' and Rhona. She had known Harry all her life; she had been brought up at Hoebridge in Melrose (a huge house with a walled garden and peach trees). She was brave, sporty, played tennis, drove and carved wood. We have a beautiful chest carved by her. Harry took Rhona on honeymoon to Norway, fishing, but she ran away. He found her at the Oslo docks.

'All day long in a small boat with only a very small sandwich to eat!' she grumbled. He then took her to the Italian Lakes and she was much happier. Honeymoons in those days were protracted affairs.

Marion was born in 1901. Betty came along in 1905 and Kenneth 2 years later whom her mother adored. She was 3 years older than Betty. Her brother and sister both said how difficult their mother found Marion as a child. But as a family before the Great War they had lived a very agreeable life.

In her old age she recounts, *(sic)*

'The summer holidays were spent at Bamburgh where they always stayed in the Old School House we went by train with two maids and a nanny and were met by a wagonette and two horses we drove along by Budle Bay, that's a lovely bay I told you about that filled up with sand and then was flooded, about six miles, the heavy luggage was left to come in a big horse drawn wagon, it took two days.

We walked such a lot on those days. Walking to Holy Island would take the whole morning, we walked 3 miles along the coast, 3 or 4 miles past the golf course. You had to go to the causeway when the tide was out and we carried our picnic, then we had to wait for the tide to go out again. There was a little village and a lovely old castle which had been built as a church on a pinnacle. It was quite tiny. Saint Aidan was supposed to be buried there. He made the Northumbrians and Celts Christians before the Saxons came. People call it Holy Island but really it is Lindisfarne.

There was no fresh fish at Bamburgh, no harbour, the fishing boats used to go to Seahouses down the coast and twice a week a cart would come with fish.

At Bamburgh we had these grass tennis courts and somebody had put in a wall and a nice 18 hole golf course, and there were lovely sandy beaches. We all learned to dive in a thing called the Egg Pool in the rocks, I suppose it must have been about 10 feet deep at the deepest end, it was lovely to dive into as it was just a sandy bottom and you couldn't get hurt. It was cleaned out twice a day by the sea. (sic)

Life had been so happy. The mill was just down the hill from their house. Harry saw a lot of his children, the two daughters who loved him best. Their studies with their governess took but a few hours and then they were free to enjoy themselves. Later they went to The Abbey School for girls in Melrose when they were about eight or nine, a day-school until they were big enough to go to secondary school at about 12 or 13. They moved to Edinburgh in 1913 when Harry was to work at the University but the war intervened. Then Marion went to St Leonards as a boarder at St Andrews and Betty went to St Georges as a daygirl. Marion chose to leave home. Betty who loved her mother stayed as a daygirl. Marion's relationship with her mother was based on rivalry. Rhona was a woman of character athletic and brave and good looking. She could have been a suffragette, but was not quite focussed enough. Marion was not so good looking. She was tall, skinny and short sighted. But she was clever and she was more athletic than her mother Mary Ann later played tennis at Wimbledon and she was ambitious and very competitive. She was of course better educated than Rhona and did not hesitate to demonstrate it. But she was very hurt by Rhona's love for Betty who was non-confrontational, placid and easy-going, she was short, fat and pretty. Rhona would say to Marion, "Betty needs expensive clothes, but you can wear anything!" Most people would not mind having that said to them, some certainly would love it, but Marion being very sensitive took great exception to this attitude and gradually built up a phobia about smart clothes, she always looked immaculate, painted her nails and indeed spent a lot of money on clothes. She was aware that she was not pretty, but she used to say to me, 'I was never pretty, but I was always crisp and clean!'

When she came home from St Leonards for the holidays – her mother would tease,

"How long are you home from school for? – Not a whole month!" Rhona would laugh, but Marion did not think it was teasing, she was bitterly hurt and repeated it over and over to us through the years! She said she threw her school report out of the train window because it was so bad, and her mother never even asked her for it!

She really felt her mother did not love her, in fact she said,

The echo again

"My mother hated me, she loved the other two! She never left me anything, she left it all in trust to you children, and the others signed her Will! The injustice of it!"

We all know the truth now, she was generous, but not improvident which is wasteful, although to her dying day she did not understand. She had always had enough money, never had to scrimp and save and could not understand her family who she thought worshipped it, because they did save. But not enough.

They did not modernise their factories and in the depression of 1929, rather than lay off workers, were bankrupted.

Harry went to War in 1915, he did not have to join up, he was 40 with a wife and three children, but he did. He joined the Royal Field Artillery, not a local regiment which would have been more friendly. His letters to his daughter Betty portray a kind loving father who longed for home.

After Betty's death in January 1992 I found remnants of family paraphernalia including her father's letters from the front.

Betty was the family hoarder! This was owing to her having no children of her own. She kept everything; little notebooks of daily expenses dating from 1947. A notebook of all the books she had read borrowed from library with A, B, C – or + against them. She kept lists of all the Christmas presents she gave and received and all the cards and thank you letters, some are very interesting. She left many books on archaeology and ancient history. She kept all the photographs MA had sent her over the years with writing on the back to explain what she had been doing. These I have used to plot her trip to Afghanistan. There are a few family letters, some dating from 1853 and 1866, one of which is reproduced below. There are others in Appendix 2.

11.2.1915

My dear Betty,

I am sorry I can't tell you where I am in France as it is not safe to send names of places through the post lest the Germans should find out where we are, so the army authorities prohibit it. We are in a very quiet little village just now very rustic and peaceful and one would never imagine that there was any war about except for the occasional distant roar of big guns and the flights of aeroplanes overhead.

Our food all comes from England and is not much different from yours except that there is not much variety about it. Roast (bully)beef potatoes bread butter jam tea and bacon every day. Sometimes we fry eggs, tinned fruit and sardines to give it variety, but we are always so hungry we don't really care very much what we eat. Of course we all smoke a great deal. So far I have not had a French meal and have not had any such luxury as frog's legs.

Today we were inspected by a great General and started out very early in the morning in pitch darkness and sleet. It sleeted and rained all forenoon so we all got soaked through and stood for hours shivering in the mud. This afternoon we are taking a half holiday to dry out our clothes. The General had a look at us through the window of his motor car, but did not trouble to stop it.

This is however the first really wet day we have had and all together our experience of France has been very pleasant. Of course we are all very anxious to get our guns going and I don't suppose it will be very long before we do.

I hope your play went off well and made a lot of money for the soldiers Fund. It would be good fun for the girls who took part in it in any case.

Write me lots of letters and I shall always endeavour to reply to them. It will be lonely living in a dug out all day and I shall probably have lots of time to write.

Love from your own Daddy.

In 1913 the family moved to Edinburgh, Marion to St Leonards at St Andrews and Betty to St Georges.

She said her mother hated her, perhaps she was jealous of her. Mary Ann was outstandingly confident. She was a brilliant tennis player although the baby book shows a picture of Rhona playing tennis there are none of her daughter who really was good. She was an intrepid climber and climbed all the Cairn Gorms, when she told her mother she refused to believe her. Though Betty and Kenneth had very composed temperaments and were rather dull, their mother adored them, they were no trouble. Marion was very sensitive and immoderate. One can imagine in the early years that her Nanny would remove her from the room when she felt twinges of envy at any attention Betty and Kenneth were getting. This made her more and more resentful of her brother and sister. Her governess was her saviour, she would take the intractable child and show her books and stories, wonderful illustrations by Heath Robinson of the History of England, with hideous deaths and deeds of valour. Mary Ann who was highly intelligent took to books. Rhona felt that Betty was just as talented (who later went on to study modern languages at Grenoble) was not getting her fair share of attention and she was so pretty and so sweet and undemanding! After all she had never been the centre of attention. Betty admired her elder sister a great deal although she was away at boarding school.

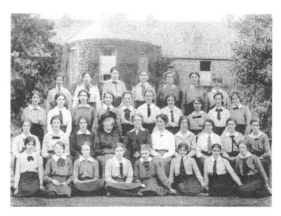

House photo of St Leonards about 1914. Marion Sanderon is sitting in the front, second from the left, with a bow rather than a tie!

She hated St Leonard's at St Andrews. She only stayed two years and after the death of her father she wanted to go home. It was freezing in winter and they had a long way to walk to church on Sundays. She said her housemistress hated her. Rhona came to tell her personally that Harry had been killed. She was surprised and very grateful. Poor Rhona had been sent all Harry's effects, his bloodied uniform full of bullet holes, watch etc. He had been shot by a sniper when climbing a tree to see where their artillery shells had landed. Although she had many friends, she begged her mother to let her leave and join Betty at St Georges which she did. At St Georges, the school has records of her there from 1916 till 1917 when she left to go to a 'small boarding school'. This was St Margaret's, Falkirk. The school no longer exists so there are no records of this, but her entry to Cambridge says she came from St. Margaret's, Polmont, Falkirk. It was not far from Edinburgh. Whilst at school in Edinburgh for two years she had a little dog, a wire-haired terrier called 'Patches'. She belonged to the local tennis club, living with her mother and Betty and Kenneth, she always helped with the family shopping. Later on when at Cambridge she remembered bringing friends home after tennis and using her father's claret from the cellar and mixing it with lemonade to make sangria. One day she was on the tram and met her dog on it, the bus conductor told her that it often took the tram up to Princes Street Gardens had a walk one supposes and went back again, on the tram to 49 Northumberland Street!

One assumes that the move from a good school like St George's to St Margaret's must have been prompted by some discord at home, but that was not necessarily so, Maths was her downfall. St George's insisted on it for the Cambridge exam, but the Headmistress of St Margaret's, a Miss Constance Worsfold, a very well regarded woman and much admired in the teaching world, would have encouraged Marion to go to Cambridge. She allowed her to give up Maths and take up Latin instead, and Mary Ann told us, her children, that as a schoolgirl she read Virgil for pleasure! Miss Worsfold must have loved her, and have been an inspiring mentor to a young girl in stressful circumstances.

She took a scholarship and got an exhibition to Cambridge. She went to an interview there and got in, but afterwards, instead of going straight back to school, she absconded! She went to stay with Aunty Kitty Tippetts, her favourite aunt in London. It was June and Kitty and her husband Percy took Marion to Henley, Wimbledon, and Ascot and gave her a lovely time. When she got back to Edinburgh her furious mother met her at Waverly Station telling her she had been expelled! She had missed all the school tennis matches, and she was tennis captain! She had let down Miss Worsfold! Her being expelled from St Margaret's must have been a shock to Rhona and added to the discord. In those days expulsion was a very serious affair, in later life when she was a struggling single mother and teacher, she was terrified that, I, her daughter should be expelled from the Royal School as all my friends were. She said she did not care, and at the time I don't expect she did, but her mother made a huge fuss and Miss Worsfold would have been very hurt and cross.

She loved Cambridge. She read History at Newnham, played in tennis tournaments and there is a photo of her in the tennis team and her game is mentioned in the magazine saying she should do more 'lobbing' of her opponents on the tennis court and she is mentioned in the debating society every month. It would have been a very exciting period with the Russian revolution etc. The subjects they debated were nothing to do with politics. I have put a + or – to denote how she voted.

'Complete toleration would be a retrograde step in civilization.' –

'Cinema in its present state is pernicious.' –

'Art and literature can flourish only in a community where there is a leisured class.' +

'Truth in Journalism is not a virtue.' –

'The Tatler is a more edifying publication than the Herald.' +

M V Sanderson was not interested in politics. When interviewed on the radio by Veronica Cecil in 1989 about 'Woman's Rights' and suffragettes she said she was only interested in fun and having a good time. After losing her father and so many friends from her childhood in the Great War, the 1920's must have been a time of relaxation for the intelligentsia.

Newnham College Tennis Team, M V Sanderson is the only one with a more flattering collar.

She rode a motorbike, she would travel up and down to Scotland on it. She played tennis, lacrosse and dived for Cambridge and should have got 2 half blues but there is no record. She joined the mountaineering Club and climbed the Cairn Gorms. Her uncle Ernest Rutherford was splitting the atom at Cavendish lab and she used to visit him and his wife.

She evidently had friends from St Leonard's, being Scottish and local and six years after she had left, the following extract of an article appeared in the St.Leonard's Gazette.

Dear Editor,

We thought we might take the readers of this Gazette a personally conducted tour round Newnham, pointing out features of note as we go. Starting then from Old Hall we come to a room on the ground floor. Here we shall find Marion Sanderson, surrounded by all her possessions at once, tea trays, hats, pyjamas, books. She is seated on her bed last made a week ago, in immaculate attire and quite unperturbed by the chaos which greets our eyes. But strange to say we too forget our surroundings under the influence of her enchanting smile and we leave the room feeling that Marion at any rate is always pleased to see us, she has found at last in Cambridge a milieu for her wonderful social gifts.

SLS GAZETTE JUNE 1922

When she graduated her mother could not or would not afford to pay for the M.A., but she got a 2.2 in History.

In the 1920's there were no men. They had all been killed in the war, but accounts of Mary Ann in those days by Kitty's son Berry, was of a dashing, cheerful, fizzy personality. She must have used all her pent up sexual energy which would otherwise have been dissipated on love, on climbing mountains, playing in tennis tournaments, getting jobs and having adventures. She had always loved horses and worked as a groom for friends in Northumberland where she rode a great deal. She played in tennis tournaments in Wimbledon, Cannes and Le Touquet.

She and some fellow students even went to Russia after the Revolution to find out and report on the new regime, foolishly they went down to the docks and landed up in prison in St Pietersburg. She also went to Canada to visit Spencer Sanderson and cousins.

The Sanderson family of Galashiels had lost all their money. The great houses where they had lived were pulled down because of the cost of running them, the mills were closing and Northumberland Street the last refuge. The family was dispersed round the world.

Kitty Tippets, née Rutherford, Rhona's younger sister, was married to Percy and was a staunch supporter of 'Merian', as she always called her. Her husband died quite early on and Kitty supported herself and Berry by playing big game poker. She had been taught by Percy who had given her a large sum of money the first year of their marriage. But she blew it and he was most upset but reimbursed her. She had learned her lesson and never really lost again. She had her income from his legacy, but became really quite rich in her own right. Throughout the War she stayed in her flat in the City of London. She played poker at Crockfords in Curzon Street for years. Mary Ann and Henry stayed with her after their marriage, she was very fond of them. There is a ditty my mother told me.

Kitty was so pretty, Kitty was so witty,
The fellows in the city tried to pull her leg,
One of the Committee, trying to be witty,
Hit her on the titty with a hard-boiled egg!

This was very naughty and not a bit like her!

When I knew her in 1960 she had a sumptuous flat in Draycott Avenue and a housekeeper called Edith, I once saw a beautiful presentation box of liqueurs in her hallway and she told me it was for a friend off whom she had won a lot of money! That's how they behaved in those days. She was shy and retiring which belied her Scottish acumen for making money. She would take the bus up to Hyde Park Corner, go to Crockfords in Curzon Street, play poker at £10 a rise and bridge until the early hours, then home by taxi, she said she did not like playing with Jews because they lied! She stayed in bed all morning talking to her stockbroker on the telephone.

Every winter she would go to Monte Carlo for two months with friends. They stayed in a small hotel The Balmoral and played *Chemmy* (Chemin de Fer) and poker at the Casino. They always saved the rolls and cheese from breakfast for their lunch. A Scottish foible! Edith would sometimes redecorate the flat whilst she was away.

Henry had given her a lamp made out of a camel's stomach, which she always pointed out to me when I visited her, it had a lovely gentle deep yellow glow.

She would sometimes send Mary Ann cheques when she had done well at poker with an accompanying note saying 'I had a good year', and we would go on holiday with it. She was like a fairy godmother to my mother over the years. She was my Godmother and in 1959 gave me £500 in lieu of a coming out dance! I gave most of it to my mother. She was so generous! She died in 1980, and left me little home-made silk lampshades, some square saucepans and two nice pictures (Clayton Adams)! She had bought an annuity so could not leave Mary Ann anything!

I digress.

In 1924 Marion set off on her peregrinations around the Empire to visit her uncles and her first stop was South Africa to teach at the Herschel School in Cape Town who paid her passage. However, it was a disaster, she hated it and left after half a term and had to pay back the cost of the boat ticket! Her mother sent her the return fare home, but of course she did not return. She went to work for the Cape Argus Newspaper in Cape Town. She enjoyed that and used to report big events and on the clothes people wore to important functions, she also reported the races.

There were many stories of her life in South Africa, at one time she stayed with a family whose father was in charge of the snakes at the Zoo. During the cold weather, and Cape Town can be quite cold, he used to take the pythons out of their enclosures because they were curled up and hibernating, to clean the enclosure, and he stored them in his attic. Well one day the Cleaner was up there cleaning and one of them woke up. Well the Cleaner found that the door would not open and so she rattled it hard to get attention, this woke up the other snake, both of them were quite sleepy and slow although they must have been very hungry. The attic was large and airy with windows and the woman went round and round, banging on the window then rattling the door with the two huge pythons following her, someone eventually saw her and came up and opened the door and let her out!

Then my mother moved to Pietermaritzberg to Epworth School. She had a farmer friend at Mooi River, Reggy Garland, she told of driving into town to the cinema at night in Mooi River and finding all the chickens still sitting on the front bumper of the car! She was very happy in South Africa she rode, played tennis and climbed the Drakensburg Mountains. She always supported herself either teaching or working for a newspaper.

During this time she says she got married but never disclosed the name. He had been shell-shocked in the Great War, now-a-days it is called post-traumatic stress disorder and they went to his farm in Marandellas in Rhodesia. She says he got drunk one night and pulled a gun on her. She packed her saddle bag and rode off into the night! That's all we know!

She was five years in South Africa and travelled around a great deal. The trains were very good and she was on a station one day bound for Johannesburg and some fellows asked her if she would like to go croc shooting on the Zambezi, so she *wired* Joberg (sent a telegram), which was so easy with the telegraph and went off to Livingstone with them.

'We just dug a hip-hole and slept on the ground'.(sic)

It was during this time that she would have been in touch with her uncle Robert Sanderson who had gone out to South Africa at the turn of the century and traveled up as a pioneer to Rhodesia just after Cecil Rhodes defeated Lobengula, chief of the Matabele tribe. Robert Sanderson was living near Bulawayo. He had a dairy farm and his daughter is Heather Valentine's mother, Mrs Johnston. Heather's husband Richard Valentine who died in 1988 had been my husband Jonathan's best friend since 1953 when they were at school together in Rhodesia and South Africa. Mrs. Johnson was a great character, very tough and horsy. She decided to slim only when she discovered she could no longer crawl in underneath her land-rover! Heather on the other hand is very slim and elegant but equally tough, she is a very talented artist. We have stayed on their beautiful farm in Odzi dozens of times. She still farms in Zimbabwe (now in 2009). She and her son Phil have given half their farm to the local Chief, all their cattle have been taken and they get robbed every other week. All their dogs get poisoned. But they are still there. (Heather died in 2010.) Phil Valentine, her son and his wife are still farming and his sister and brother-in-law Kassy and John Robbie, live in Harare, they import and sell medicines and prophylactics (2017). Sadly neither Mary Ann nor Richard Valentine knew of our connection. They would both have been so thrilled had they known!

In 1928 my mother returned to Edinburgh. It may have been because Betty had broken her leg and was in hospital for months. Rhona would have sent her the boat ticket.

In 1929 she went by boat to New Zealand to visit her Rutherford cousins. On the boat a trans-gender man stole all her clothes and in Australia after swimming in Sydney harbour, she was told it was full of sharks! She got a position teaching at the Diocesan School in Auckland. She taught History to 15 year olds, her favourite subject and loved it. She stayed with her uncle David who farmed at Masterson. She tells how early in her stay, one night coming in from riding she kicked her boots into the corner of the kitchen and in the morning they were still there! Very different from life in South Africa! She loved New Zealand she climbed Mt Cook and worked as a ski-instructor there, she tells of an avalanche and how she could not tell which way up she was, then she remembered to dribble! She learned to fly in a Bristol Fighter. She was the first woman to fly the Cook Straight in an AVRO 504. She had a boyfriend who lived on an island and she used to fly over to join him at weekends. She also knew the Chichester family, their son was the first man to circumnavigate the world single handed. She stayed in New Zealand some years returning to Scotland in about 1932.

In all those years of travelling and working there must always have been a lack of men in her life. I don't know much about her life in those years because I was born in 1941. But she was always able to get a job, she was responsible and reliable, she had to be as she was extravagant and generous. She had been working in Switzerland from 1932 -33 she taught at La Casta, Lausanne. It was during this period that she went to a rally in Vienna and heckled Hitler and was hustled away by the furious crowd in disgrace, that's what she told us! She had been staying with a friend from Cambridge who had become a nun!

She was shocked by her acceptance of Hitler's occupation of the Rhine lands. She writes about staying there.

'I was there for 2 months in – I think 1932 – staying at St Maximin with a girlfriends' family. She later became a nun when her boyfriend – in the French Army – let her down. So Sad. I visited her years later at her convent at Amiens and talked through the grille. She was so pretty and amusing. So very sad. The family home was in Draguignan and people still got their water from the village well and of course no plumbing. They lived in a high town house – several hundred years old with stone floors upstairs.

He (her father) was a doctor, some sort of specialist who visited patients. He had killed a man and lost his driving license and made me drive him through those little lanes, but well away from town he took the wheel. I have never been more frightened. But they were all so nice and funny. He had a surgery in Cannes and kept a little sailing boat there. And we went to Corsica in it and stayed for a few days, also perilous crossings.'

She went to India in about 1934 or 35. She will have visited her family in Edinburgh many times during these years. They would have been pleased to see her but they gave her nothing, except return boat fares. After the depression life had been hard for them. Her mother lived in Edinburgh with Kenneth, and her friends were his friends.

Betty married Jack Purves during the war, she was a FANNY, he was in the Royal Scots. After the War they lived in Edinburgh. Back in 1926 when she was 19, Betty broke her leg very badly and Mary Ann came home. I expect her mother paid her fare. Betty had a weak bone in her leg and had to have grafts taken from her spine to mend it. Over the years she broke her leg over and over again in the same place. It got shorter and shorter. Betty was short and stout, nevertheless she played golf until she was over 60. She and her husband, Jack Purves never had any children, but they loved their nephew George and wanted to adopt him!

Jack had been in the army and much later after the war he became Secretary of the Gosforth Park Golf Club in Newcastle, where people still remember him.

Kenneth had a sad life. He was the first Sanderson child in to be educated out of Scotland. He went to Winchester College from 1922 -26. He had a great affection for Winchester and became an expert on the Cathedral and more knowledgeable than the vergers! He had always wanted to be an architect. His mother had thwarted him and instead he read Law at Edinburgh

University and became a WS (Writer of the Signet). In the war he joined the Royal Navy as a Writer and served in the West Indies. Afterwards he lived with her and worked as a bursar in girls' schools. But when he was young he had had a budding relationship with a girl who lived in Northern Ireland and he used to go there on holiday and they played tennis together and walked. When war was declared he probably did not write to her enough. He was away a lot and her parents came over to Edinburgh to ask Rhona what Kenneth's intentions were. Rhona sent them off saying he had no intentions and no money and was not thinking of marrying their daughter! The girl became a nun and entered a convent. Kenneth was shocked when he returned from the navy to discover this. However no more was heard from her until many years later he got a letter from the convent/monastery to say she had died and left him all her money! Kenneth gave it to the convent!

After the war Kenneth lived at 29 Northumberland Street with Rhona. He worked in girls' schools and was interested in fine china and old buildings. He retired to Darnick, Melrose and played bridge. He had a very comfortable life with a housekeeper called Miss Sheather who ruled the roost.

There are some stories about Miss Sheather. When she retired she took the carpet from her room with her!

She gave away, or sold the autograph book/ photo album with all the family photos to an American whose wife nee' Sanderson was looking for her Sanderson ancestors. We only know this because the book was returned to Scotland by the American

Everyone laughed about it, this little book had been all over America and no one could recognize their relations, so it was sent back to Elizabeth Sanderson in Edinburgh.

The letter that came with the photo album

9 East Fettes Avenue, Edinburgh EH4 1DN

20th Feb 1989

Dear Mrs Storey,

By a very strange chance I have been sent by a friend in America a photograph album to see if I can identify any of the people in it who all belong to Galashiels, Mrs Purves's childhood home. To my amazement I find that the album belongs to Mrs Purves's mother so there are a number of photo's Mrs Purves herself as a child, also her sister and brother and of course her parents. Her father was killed in the First World War and was one of my father's younger brothers. There are two very good photos of him. I am therefore writing to ask you if you think Mrs Purves would recognize any of these pictures as if so, though it is rather a large and heavy volume, I will gladly send it to her to keep. If any of the photos do stir her memory it would of course be excellent.

Thanking you again for all your kindness to her

Yours sincerely

Elizabeth Sanderson

PS I enclose a stamped addressed envelope for your reply. Is Mrs Purves's sister Marian still alive and if so would you please let me know her address, as if Mrs Purves does not want the photos, perhaps she would.

8 East Fettes Ave, Edinburgh

6th March, 1989.

My dear Betty,

This is just a note to enclose with the photo album which was recently sent to me by an old friend in the USA whose wife is a distant relation of the 'Skinbrocks' in Galashiels, as we used to call them. This Clayton Ford and his wife, Lois went to Galashiels to find out all they could of this relationship about 12 years ago but I never heard of the photo album until now. But I will write and ask him how he got hold of it and tell him that the photos are mostly of your relations. The ones of your father are very good. I of course remember him clearly as my Uncle Harry. No doubt you will also remember the children at the end of the book with whom you must have played. I also remember the delightful holiday your mother gave my mother and me at Bamburgh of which there are several good photos.

I will let you know when I hear from Clayton how he obtained the book.

I am so glad you are now recovering so well from your recent illness.

With love and best wishes as ever from your cousin,

Elizabeth Sanderson

Please thank Mrs Story for her kind letter and give her my kind regards and thanks.

The Photo Album remains here amongst MA's photos. Proper photos are now a rarity, there are lots of pictures of Harry's guns and members of his regiment all put there lovingly by Rhona. It was a wicked thing for Miss Sheather to do, Kenneth would not have known it was missing.

In their later years, Kenneth, Mary Ann and Betty were very good friends. They used to go on holiday together which Kenneth would organize. They went on cruises to exotic places and saw many lovely castles and ruins. They always took a mutual friend who would make up the bridge four in the evenings.

Chapter 4

India

1930-36

DURING THESE YEARS my mother returned to Scotland at least twice when Betty broke her leg. She worked in Geneva for a time and at La Casita, Lausanne and did a lot of climbing in her spare time, she climbed the Matterhorn and the Weisshorn.

She visited Austria where her Uncle Frank, a retired Judge from Egypt had settled in Vienna. In Vienna they attended a rally and she heckled Hitler and was hustled out of the crowd in disgrace! These were the stories I heard over and over as she entertained her admiring friends, it was all so long ago and I've forgotten most of them.

In 1932 or 33, in the tradition of the great British *fishing fleet* (husband hunting), Marion Sanderson went to India to stay with friends in Peshawar. Her friends were Dorothy (nee Haydon) and Pip Crouch, earlier Dorothy Haydon who she had played tennis with at Wimbledon, Dorothy had been a regular Wimbledon player. She did not stay with Dorothy long because she moved into a hotel near the Club. Together with a trained Froebel teacher, they started a school, the friend teaching the pre-school and Mary Ann teaching the older children. The school ran from October until April, when it became too hot and everybody went up to a hill station in Kashmir. So she was free from April till October and would go climbing in the nearby Himalayas. This was her life for about 3 years.

Peshawar was a centre for Government administration. There was a huge British population there mainly Indian Army. The winters were mild and pleasant.

That first year in Peshawar Mary Ann met Eddie Fluett who was a local District Commissioner (administrator in the Indian Civil Service) and a climber. In the summer holidays when her school was closed she used to visit his district and watch him paying his labour force. She considered him to be a very good administrator and a good friend but no more than that. She suspected him of being homosexual and as a result had an open easy friendship which took her to his district to wait for him to be free and to arrange guides and horses for the next trip up into the hills. He would tour the fortified villages where he would talk to the headmen. He spoke the local languages and dialects which changed the further they went into Tibet. The villages were enclosed by high mud walls with towers at the corners rather like small forts which in reality they were, as people were and still are, always having blood feuds with their neighbours. The houses and villages were all fortified. The people were paid by the British Government not to fire across the road and heavily fined if they did.

During her first two years in Peshawar there were many such expeditions and treks. They would hire ponies and also took the odd sheep with them which they butchered and ate. Once they went to Mardan and en route called at the Lawley's bungalow, and went to see the Guides Cavalry Memorial Chapel. With Eddie Fluett she went to Tibetan monasteries, at one, a dead snow leopard hanging over the entrance with the innards still in, dripped maggots! When climbing mountains, sometimes they had no tents and then would dig snow holes to sleep in at night to keep out of the wind. The sleeping bag was fur-lined. She was the first single woman up Kolahoi in July 1935. She climbed it alone with a sherper. The other members of the party had had to turn back as their leave was up. The whole expedition had been postponed by 3 days of wet weather. There were very many stories about climbing and many expeditions with friends. Walking in the mountains was very popular with incredible views in beautiful pristine countryside.

Photography was one of Marion Sanderson's pastimes, she won competitions for her mountain 'scapes.

42

On one expedition she was with her Sherpa and they were due to meet Eddie and the main expedition who had the food. They waited a night and when there was no sign of him they climbed the peak. They had had nothing to eat but hoped he would have arrived by the time they were back. When they returned after climbing the peak a day later he was still not there, but a messenger arrived to say he was held up and she must go down. So for 3 days she and the Sherpa had no food, but they got down in the end.

She took a girl-friend climbing and they had to eat baked beans all the time because her husband would not allow them to have them at home!

Trekking in Himalayas

Trekking in Himalayas

In about 1934 when she was on leave from the school, she went off to Afghanistan with a man called Ken, who was Military Attaché to the Governor Sir George Cunningham and his bearer. It was a very exciting expedition. They stayed in Kabul and at a dinner at the British Legation (embassy) she was asked what the most impressive thing she had seen, 'The British Legation of course!' she said which was a good reply as it was referred to by Curzon as worth two divisions! They were staying there as he was on an official trip for the British Government. Ken's remit was to find out if the Russians were putting in petrol dumps for a future invasion! It was a continuation of 'The Great Game'. Russia and Germany were allies after all and remained so until well after the outbreak of war.

She took a lot of photographs on the expedition, there are photos of the Lundi Kotal Khyber Pass, Jalalabad on the way to Kabul the Kabul River Gorge. There are lots of photos of the legation and the huge grand car they travelled in together. 'The Afghans are ghastly, they always spat at me.' She wrote. There is a photo of Mary Ann in a dress standing in front of an Afghan soldier and on the reverse of the photo she writes '*soldier turns his back on me*'! They went down the Ghorband valley and met a great camel caravanserai carrying bales of carpets south from Kabul.

The Buddha, Barbers Tomb at Bamian, Ken.

Then north to Bamian which is 100 miles east and slightly north of Kabul a long journey where the houses were built in the rock like caves. There are photographs of the Babar's tomb, and another taken from inside the top of it with an incredible view. The two Buddha's have recently been destroyed by the Taliban.

The view of Bamian from inside the top of the tomb.

They went down the Kabul River on a raft and had adventures in the floods, there is a photo of Ken with a jersey round his waist because his shorts and stockings got wet and had to be dried before they could go on. The official car always in the background. It must have been a very exciting adventure, and all recorded on the backs of photos sent to Betty in Edinburgh. They had many punctures and hold ups, it was an intrepid expedition with Ken's bearer in tow.

Old walls round Kabul City.

46

Sentry turns his back.

Village in Bamian Valley.

Bamian Buddha.

47

Floods at Hagar, Ken's shorts got wet.

Srinagar.

When they returned to Peshawar everyone was surprised that they were unscathed. (Except I suspect that she had had to have a secret abortion)

This trip must have been in September 1934 before she met Henry.

In the winter months she taught. She belonged to the club, played tennis, golf and bridge and of course in time met Henry there.

It was one of the happiest times of Mary Ann's life, extremely social because there were so many British there and had been for decades. She used to go hunting with the Peshawar Vale Hunt jumping over the banks and ditches, hunting jackals. She was lent a pony called *Grenadine* by a Grenadier Guard obviously. There was always a large contingent of officers in Peshawar in those days and not many in commerce (boxwallahs)! She played tennis with Dorothy and with Muriel Lowis (Jonathan's aunt), they went for treks into the mountains had lots of picnics and masses of parties. In the photographs, the women climbing in the snow wore divided skirts above the knee, they all did. Nobody worried about upsetting the locals, they all respected each other, Muslims, Hindus or Sikhs, they must have been inured to half naked British memsahibs!

In Srinagar after one party she found a coiled up gabardine mackintosh belt in her bed, put there as a joke, (to look like a snake), she fainted dead away. She shared a houseboat with an old friend Christina Forbes Dalrymple from Scotland known as Chris (more about her later).

Mary Ann met and became good friends with a woman, another member of the *Fishing Fleet* who was called Jennifer McCormack. She was visiting her uncle who ran the hospital and staying with D C. She was looking for lodgings. Mary Ann at that time was living in the Deans Hotel and working in the school. Jennifer could not continue to stay with the C's. D made Jennifer's position in the household invidious, D wanted to go out to the club in the evenings to enjoy herself and her husband did not, and she wanted Jennifer to stay behind with her husband Pip and entertain him! So when Jennifer met Mary Ann and told her, they decided to share the hotel room. So she shared her twin bedded hotel room with Jennifer and nobody knew! Mary Ann paid full board anyway. They evidently tipped the bearer well and made friends with him and Jennifer moved into the bedroom with Mary Ann. Jennifer went out to lunch every day with her uncle at the hospital and so Mary Ann had the hotel lunch, then Jennifer had the hotel dinner. This arrangement continued for about 6 months in fact whilst Mary Ann met and was wooed by Henry Pelly and Jennifer tells how she persuaded Mary Ann to accept him. She said that he was the best looking man in Peshawar, but her, Mary Ann's natural modesty; assumed she was much too old for him, 9 years to be exact. She always said that the marriage would never last and that he was bound to go off with someone much younger and prettier than her. She pretended to others to be indifferent to him perhaps as a defence against the day he might leave her, but really she was very much in love with him. Jennifer remained a great friend all her life and told me about Henry in 1993, after Mary Ann was dead!

Mary Ann and Jennifer kept in touch all their lives. Jennifer returned to England before the outbreak of war. She later married a Pole who was over in England with the Polish Army during the war. Jennifer was asleep in the corner of a railway carriage and he drew her. That was how they met! He later became a well-known and recognized artist Ruzcowski and they had three children. He died last year 1992.

Mary Ann met Henry in about 1936 in Peshawar. They went to the Club a lot, he loved music and dancing she hated it, and would spend the evenings at the bar, talking. She told me Indian officers were allowed in the Club, but they never brought their wives. She worked at her school, hunted, played tennis and went climbing. Henry did none of these things. She lived in her hotel at this time and sharing with Jennifer.

1936 must have been a happy year perhaps the happiest of her life. Her trip with Ken was forgotten, and one assumes it must have been Ken's child. Presumably he was married and his wife at home (England). She used to say that she was caught in the snow in the mountains but in fact she probably went up to Gulmarg or somewhere after everyone had left for the plains and had it then. It may not be true. So come 1937 she met Henry in Peshawar and came home in late 1938 to marry him in Edinburgh.

I think because we teased her about being so much older than her contemporaries, she brought this child to our attention, we bullied her about being so old. Anyway she told us that she had had this baby which miscarried, it was a boy and we as children called it 'Charles'!

She seldom spoke of her life before she married Henry. She was swept off her feet by him. She went back to Scotland to think it all over.

They were married in Edinburgh on April 29th, 1939. He was 29 and she 38. War was declared on 1st September 1939. He was very good looking and she was I repeat, no beauty but Henry just loved her, she was a very good companion and she could do anything. She was very sporty and very clever and highly educated. This would have been about the time she went to the famous cookery school in Edinburgh Athol Crescent. She let people know what she thought of them. Most responded positively to her, some adored her, but some did not. She thought Henry an ignoramus,

You do not know who came first, Jesus Christ or Julius Cesar! Who did he asked?

Henry's family came from Ballycastle in Northern Ireland, his mother had been Nancy (Anne) Grove from The Manor House, Rathlin Island. Nancy was one of 8 daughters the eldest had gone to India with the *fishing fleet* to find husbands, Nancy was no exception she went to India and met Charles Brent Pelly in the Indian police service who was a graduate of Trinity Dublin and had been in Madras since 1891. They were married in 1901 and Henry had two elder siblings Betty and Charles known as Ben.

Henry had been educated at Campbell College, Belfast, played in the school band and rugby team, been a prefect and had gone to Cranwell. He had originally been destined for the Air Force, but he could not judge distance, so went to Sandhurst and joined the Indian Army instead, the largest volunteer army in the world and was posted first to Peshawar.

They went on honeymoon to Gleneagles Hotel so that they could play golf, he was a good golfer. She found the course much too long, her drives could never carry the rough, she never improved but loved the game and played all her life. Then they went to Northern Ireland to see Henry's relations.

'It's a beautiful country full of horrible people!' She would say. 'They told me NOT to go to catholic shops to buy things!' Henry's family were charming, but she always said what she thought, not the sort of thing to say in hearing of her new in-laws! She was shocked by the sectarianism of the people and Henry's propensity to scrounge. His mother Nancy Pelly, had always been poor and although they were the landed gentry owning Rathlin Island they had never had any money. Nancy had married the successful, famous Commissioner of Police in Madras, but he had taken very early retirement due to ill health, so she had a very small pension. But they were always very sweet to Mary Ann and she loved them. So Mary Ann and Henry had opposite upbringings. (She rich and he poor). She was shocked when, after staying with friends for the night Henry, filled up his car at the host's petrol pump. But in later life Henry's brother Ben and family were very good and generous to her and the Pellys were always the most favourite cousins, generous, kind and welcoming.

They returned to India as soon as War broke out. He was posted to Poona where he wrote this long interesting letter to Betty, thanking her for the wedding present, Mary Ann had evidently been very ill in Edinburgh before going out to join him.

Letter from Henry in Poona to Betty congratulating them on their marriage.

Poona

10.4.40

Dearest Betty and Jack,

It was great news hearing that you had both decided to jump off the dock and I'm glad you got our wire on the auspicious day. We thought of you and drank your health. Since then we have had your letter from St Andrews and a cheery one it was too. I envied you the golf there. The course here is quite baked up these days and play is out of the question unless one is very hard up for something to do. We had some good golf in Bombay on grass. Well we have moved into our new bungalow and though it has got some very bad faults it has also many good ones and is on the whole better than we expected. M.A. will have told you that there is only one large room and a dressing room and pantry and one bathroom. Upkeep is going to be cheap enough and that at the moment is a major consideration. It is however very hot in Poona nowadays and the smaller rooms are quite unbearable. It was fun unpacking all our gear, I actually had never seen the half of it and really I think people were most generous to us! Did you get many? I daresay you didn't as your friends and relations had little warning, but no doubt they will rally round eventually.

Little doing here in the way of 'action' in this war, at least not much that meets the eye and I'm wondering what the world and our reaction will be to Germany's action today. We all got the most tremendous surprise to hear that she had invaded Denmark and Norway as we've had no news, yet speculation is rife as to what the other neutrals such as Sweden, Holland and Belgium will do. I somehow can't see Sweden coming in on our side, though one would imagine that she'd back up Norway. She's always been pro-German and it would appear that she'll remain neutral with pro-German leanings. Holland and Belgium must have the complete wind up.

I wonder what has happened to your Norwegian friends. Hope they are alright, but we've heard that Norway is resisting so that can't be a wise proceeding. How are we going to tackle these Huns? An expeditionary force to Scandinavia or just sea and air action? By the time you get this we'll know and lets hope that we have taken immediate action.

Well, I've got a horrible job this week supervising an exam. Means sitting on my backside watching half a dozen lads for 6 hours a day. Hence this rush into print to fill in time. We had a grand leave in Bombay plenty of bathing, golf and flicks.

Poona is reasonably cheerful and we're getting to know people. M.A. doesn't know many yet but some old friends from Peshawar are here. The drawback about this place is the climate. Nobody minds the heat so long as there is a bit of cold thrown in and this is definitely the 'sloth-belt', very little variation in temp all the year round. Very dry and barren too just now. June should see the monsoon and green grass. Racing, golf etc., get cracking then and Poona gets very gay for the half of Bombay come up here then, including part of the local Government.

I have recommended to undergo a War Course at the Staff College but I've an idea that the recommendation may not go very far and in my case could not come into operation for another year or so. These courses are held at Quetta and are shorter editions of the ordinary Staff College courses.

I gather everyone at home has to do a short time in the ranks before getting a Commission and I do hope Jack's time will be as short as possible. What Rgt., is he going in to? Wonder what happened to my brother Ben yesterday in this sea battle off Norway or he may not have been there. I do so hope he gets his promotion and I know he wants a chance to show what he's worth and a bit of 'action' is the answer to that.

I do wish this war would really get a move on and we out here are only too keen to do our stuff if the Indian Govt., would let us. I've no doubt that we eventually will join in and when we do we'll be pretty strong. Perhaps the events of yesterday really mean we've started. I do hope so. Anyhow I'm talking tripe. Poor Betty, you didn't have too good a winter, long hours biting cold and illness and I reckon you're having your break now and I hope Jack is giving you a really good time. Give him a kick in the pants from me. This marriage racket is a good one though there may be the odd spot of worry, thing always turn out alright. M.A. is gradually putting on weight, she's a wonder really considering what she went through only 5 months ago. Sends you both her love of course and will surely write you again soon.

All the very best of everything to you both. May you have a happy life and a prosperous one. (Though I must say Army pay is not very conducive to the latter state!)

Give my love to Ma Sanderson too.

Yours affectionately

Henry.

From now onwards Mary Ann will be aka M.A.

This letter is the bench mark for the start of M.A's life that I know of.

Betty and Jack had a happy prosperous life, Jack died in 1971 and Betty in 1992.

As sisters Betty and MA were close, there is a store of photos with MA's writing on the back which she sent to Betty over the years from 1920's in South Africa this book is based on them.

Henry and M.A. stayed in Poona for two years and I, their first child was born there and then he was posted to Quetta, where he did a course in Desert Warfare. Then he was sent to the Eritrean battles against the Italians. In the desert he was wounded. The vehicle was blown up and he was thrown through the windscreen and the end of his nose was cut off, but stitched on again! Henry sent MA a letter, more of which I will tell later. Whilst Henry was away MA and baby went to Kashmir, Srinagar and shared a houseboat with a friend, Chris Royle whose husband was killed later at Arnhem. They also went to Gulmarg for the summer and shared a hut with Lois Roberts a good friend in later life.

The Letter

In about 1942 Henry was posted to Eritrea and into the Desert. M A was in Kashmir sharing hut with Lois. M A had Sarah aged a few months and Lois had two babies. Letters from the Desert were rare and M A was worried because Henry had been shot up in his jeep. The driver had been killed and he had gone through the windscreen and lost his nose! Anyhow all turned out well in the end and Henry's nose was sewn on again with tiny stitches and he assured her that he was just as handsome as ever! He was in fact very handsome. Well someone else thought so too! Because MA got a letter from him saying that he had fallen in love with his nurse and all was over with old Mary Ann he was going to marry this other woman who no doubt was young and pretty. M A was neither young nor pretty and she was not really terribly surprised by the letter although she was terribly worried. After all she was nine years older than Henry and this nurse could be some years younger. She might be very young and very sweet and very pretty. Not knowing what to do exactly she finished knitting a woolly scarf for him and went to the bazaar and bought a warm sheepskin waistcoat because the desert could be very cold. She finished the loving letter she had been writing to him telling him all about his daughter who was very naughty and made a large saucepan of fudge which was his favourite. With a feeling of despair she parcelled it all up and sent it off to him. Hoping it would not get lost in the post. So many letters went missing. A pity his to her had not.

A few months later Henry wrote to say he was coming to the Staff College in Quetta to do jungle training. There was no mention of the other woman! When he got back she was unpacking his suitcase and found a photo of a woman.

'Is this her?' she asked.

He was amazed, 'I thought my letter had got lost in the post,' he said. They both laughed.

Gulmarg during the war when she was married to Henry. 1942 – There were no cars

By *Lois Roberts*
(*One of her oldest friends*)

We took a taxi to Tanberg then all the stuff was carried up. The coolies who were paid an Ana went up the steepest way. We went up slowly to and fro to and fro zig zagging. The forest was thick on either side. The 'marg' or valley up top, on the edge of a high plateau where the trees give way to flowers was the hill station where people went to get away from the dust and heat of Srinagar in the summer.

On a clear day one can see 80 miles across the Kashmir valley to Nanga Parbat and the snow-capped peaks of the Himalayas rising above the mists and clouds.

In the summer 1942 when all the men were away fighting and Henry was in the Western Desert, Mary Ann left Srinagar went to Gulmarg this time with her baby. There were no cars. She shared a hut with her friend, Lois who had two babies. Mary Ann had no ayah but got one who was the daughter of Lois's ayah called 'Baghu'. Baghu was very young and had not been to Gulmarg before, she came from warmer parts. That particular year the spring was late and when they got to Gulmarg the snow was still piled up behind the huts and it was freezing. The first morning Baghu did not arrive to take the baby. Mary Ann yelled for

Baghu to come. The Bearer who had come up with them went to my mother and explained ' Baghu not come, Baghu cold ', MA was furious and asked why Baghu was cold? Bearer said 'Baghu no have coat'! Mary Ann at once realised the problem and gave Bearer her own coat to give Baghu! Lois says it was a lovely coat, but possessions meant little. She had travelled the world with nothing to show for it.

There is a photo of two men carrying a large wicker cot with a child in it. On the back is written:

'The Dooley. How S took her walks in Gulmarg. The paths are too rough for prams.
In front of the wooden shack which was our room and where the mushrooms grew.'

There was one woman who frowned on Lois and Mary Ann, they did not know why but invited her to tea, she came to tea and then she asked them back twice and they forgot twice all she said was ' ..and there were strawberries!' This was told by Lois.

Once again MA taught in the school, The Garden School in Srinagar. Her friend Mary Grove who was a Montessori teacher taught the little ones and Mary Ann taught the older girls, English and Geography. One day after a lesson she asked "Any Questions?"

A little girl put up her hand and said "Mrs Pelly, why is your face so lined?" She had never used sun-block only talcum-powder to keep off the sun.

July 1943, Wedding of Doris Lincoln in Gulmarg. MA standing front left, smoking!
Mary Grove sitting next to the bride. Mary Grove later ran Slepe Hall, St Neots 1957.

School was only in the morning. So many afternoons were spent on the tennis courts or on one of the three golf courses. MA's golf was terrible however much she played, she remained a 36 handicap! But she loved it. The evenings were often spent at the club playing bridge! She and Lois got on very well although they were very different from each other. She came flying out of the hut one day saying she'd put acetone into the baby's eyes by mistake instead of eye drops. Lois, always so calm put castor oil and cold cream into her eyes to alleviate them. Baghu then put the cold cream in the baby's hair and my mother was furious. Lois and Mary Ann talked a lot about their futures and hopes. MA was always self- deprecating, and he was so young and good looking and so much her junior, but she was quite interesting to look at, in an attractive lively way. There was nothing frowzy or frumpish about her she was always smart. Lois had hired the hut for the summer and MA agreed to pay half but suddenly got news that Henry was returning from the desert and was to go to Staff College at Quetta, with never a thought she departed. Lois was surprised that she was so thrilled to be reunited she did not realize how really and truly she adored Henry. She told me 'your mother jumped up and down and was so thrilled I was amazed at her'. Silly old Lois of course my mother was thrilled she really loved Henry. She went off so excited that she forgot to pay the rent.

Throughout the years Lois and MA remained great friends. Lowis' husband John was very unsuccessful but Lois kept their large family together, was the breadwinner and guided them through many tragedies. She had four children three girls and a boy who sadly died aged 16. From Gulmarg MA went to Quetta, first Outram Rd, then to a large bungalow in Henderson Road, her friends used to graze their horses on the lawn. They had a lovely dog, a golden retriever Sona, ('Gold' in Irdu') and George was born there. He was a tiny baby. Henry's first letter about him said, he is too small put him back!

Quetta was a very social place and life was very pleasant for the wives whilst their men were away fighting. MA worked teaching Indians English. Sarah had a pony called Lucky Boy. Henry was fighting in Burma. His letters tell of the jungle in the Arakan mountains in western Burma. He was hoping for promotion to Lt Colonel. He got it, but was killed on his way to his new posting.

1944, Family and Sona at Quetta Club. George had just been born.

1946, George with Sona.

PHOTOS OF LIFE IN INDIA AND AFGHANISTAN, CLIMBING WITH EDDIE, TRAVELLING WITH KEN:

Sherpas and ponies, climbing with Eddie.

Houseboat Srinagar

Ken and Bearer.

Kashmiri family, note the trousers!

Mary Ann on Zo

Water skiing on Dhal Lake, 1935

Picnicking.

Henry Patrick Neville Pelly, 16th Punjab Regiment.

Henry with colleagues (above and below).

Henry with his mother Nancy in Northern Ireland.

Chapter 5

COMING HOME

MARY ANN HAD to stay on in India for two long years after Henry had been killed. It had been in late January 1945, she and the children were on holiday at Menorah an island off Karachi. It was where some of the Memsahibs went to get away from the ice and snow in Quetta in winter. My father had had some leave from Burma and MA had been expecting him to get a plane across India to meet up with her at Karachi. I remember, aged 4, watching the flying-boats come in because she said he would be on one. Henry was on his way on leave from the Arakan to Menorah, but in Calcutta he had to report to HQ and they sent him off to take command of the 2nd Battalion 1st Punjab Regiment he would have been Lt. Colonel. It was his longed for promotion but, the plane a Beechcraft, with 5 passengers including General Warren crashed way off course on the Brahmaputra River. An RAF friend of Henry's later identified it by its markings. He was quite certain. Mary Ann knew that Henry would get a flying boat to Karachi and spend a few days with her and the children there. There was a muddle over her receiving the news of his death. The neighbour in Quetta had forwarded the telegram in an envelope. Henry's letters arrived direct to Menorah. So she opened them first and the neighbour's last. It was only when the telegram fell out and she compared the dates that she realized his plane had been lost en route to his new command. She got a letter later from him written the night he took off that it was pouring and blowing great guns and that he had been packing and repacking his rucksack, as he could only take one with him.

She immediately telegraphed his Headquarters to ask about the search for the plane. It was later always known as General Warren's plane. It was a calamity.

She was a very responsible and reliable person, totally in control of her life. She worked at a College in Quetta, had her own bank account decided and planned her own life. To go down to Menorah for the winter was quite an undertaking with the dog Sona and two children on the train. She went with another mother and children so was not alone.

Two years later she returned to the UK on *SS Camaronia* in January 1947 aged 46. She had been living in Quetta for the past four years and worked at a college for young Indian women teaching English. George and Sarah were now 2 and 5. George, who was born in Quetta, had been in hospital having his bandy legs straightened and Sarah as usual had been a she-devil. There is a great litany of the terrible things I did including losing the silver teapot into the drain beside the road. Mary Ann was having a bath after a day out climbing, when Bearer called through the bathroom door,

"Memsahib! Did you take the silver teapot with you?" I had been playing with it in the drain outside the garden. They had a bungalow and large garden at 18 Henderson Road in Quetta, there are photos with friends' horses grazing the lawn and a golden retriever called Sona, whom she adored; her solace.

When George was a baby they always knew where he was, because Sona's tail could be seen as she followed him loyally about through the shrubs and long grass. When eventually they left, the dog was not allowed on the ship. But dogs were allowed on troop ships so, MA arranged for a soldier to bring Sona home on a troop ship. He was paid and the fare was paid, but he never delivered her, and even though she wrote to his commanding officer she never heard of Sona again. He must have sold her to an Indian.

It was a very unhappy voyage for MaryAnn Pelly. She was the only widow on board, everyone else had their husband and she had had to leave her lovely Karen (Burmese) nanny in India. I was very difficult, had always had nannies and was quite wild. It was said that I threw MA's glasses and false teeth overboard! I don't remember that, but I do remember being beaten for stealing sweets from the next door cabin. George was forever getting lost. Once was found going up and down in the food lift to the kitchen a sort of dumb-waiter. It must have been a hideous time for her, but she had friends on board whom she had known in Quetta and Kashmir.

The ship went to Glasgow where the little family were met by 'Ma Sanderson', Rhona and brother Kenneth who took them back to 29 Northumberland Street, Edinburgh. A nanny was found for the children and a school for 'she-devil' round the corner. In fact I never went; they discovered me in the 'basement area' playing with the cook's children. Mary Ann thought she might get a job and stay a while as it was a large roomy house with a top floor for the children. But it did not work out as we children were very naughty and Kenneth could not bear the sticky finger marks on the furniture. He found his mother ironing her sheets dry one night because someone had emptied a carafe of water over the bed! So MA decided she should leave. She applied for a job where she could take the two children with her. Her first job was at a boarding school in Bishop Sutton, Arlesford, where she was able to take them both. There was a very nice woman working there called Mildred Nicholas with two little daughters, Tessa and Jane. Her husband, Tom had been in the Navy and had bought up large amounts of land in Wales after the war and was broke. Mildred worked in the school as a teacher and shared a Nissan hut with MA. They became great friends and later they would have wonderful holidays at their farm, Bryncothi in Carmarthenshire.

The Bishop Sutton job did not last long so MA then got a position in London at Harrow School for Girls leaving me at Bishops Sutton. She got to know Miss Knowles there who later took me to France for the summer to a family called Poidatz hoping to teach me French. It was very kind of her to help MA in this way. MA worked as a house mistress and taught English and History. George went to stay with her sister Betty Purves who lived in London with husband Jack. Betty & Jack adored George (they wanted to adopt him) and MA would come to see him at weekends. George was an adorable baby, fat and happy. He was admired whilst sitting on Betty's knee in a bus,

"What a lovely baby you have!" She replied, "He's my sister's, but you are a little bit mine aren't you?"

"No, I am all Mummy's," was George's emphatic reply.

At this time Mary Ann a single mother, lived a wandering existence, spending the holidays in hotels or with relations and friends such as the Nicholas's which was very difficult. But Henry's brother Ben and his wife Caroline Pelly who lived near Weymouth were staunch supporters of MA and the children. They had a lovely old rectory called The Elms in Chickerall with about 8 bedrooms and a single bathroom with a huge garden and orchard. Also there were cousins, Jane, Paddy and Will. Ben Pelly had been cashiered out of the Navy for riding his bicycle round the edge of the billiard table and after the War worked raising money for the Cancer Campaign. He did not make much money and the family was always struggling. Will was the same age as me and we would all go to The Elms every year for Christmas. Ben & Henry's mother old Granny Nancy Pelly, an inveterate scrounger, who was very religious was nearly always there too and she waged a war on Jean's cats. Jean was Caroline's sister who had a flat in the house and about 15 cats. The cats were a scourge and the flat behind a baize door reeked. We had a wonderful time with Will building dens and generally having fun with all the goings on. Jane was young and beautiful and there were lots of parties with young men from the naval base, Portland. She eventually married one, Ken Mills and they took on The Elms. It now has about 6 bedrooms and 5 bathrooms.

Apart from relations MA knew very few people in England after all that time abroad in New Zealand, South Africa and India, apart from the few people from the Indian Army now based at Larkhill in Wiltshire. So she applied for a job in Salisbury at the Salisbury & South Wilts Grammar School and with her father's little bit of money bought a semi-detached house, 38 Wordsworth Road on the high hill above the school. Replacing the head of English who had gone on a sabbatical was a major challenge. She said she had never worked so hard in her life. She had to walk up to Wordsworth Road with bags of books to correct. But she got a car eventually and life began to take shape. The children went to Leaden Hall School in Salisbury where she met Lucy Hughes who was the cook with her son Anthony the same age as George. She also worked at Manor School, Durnford where she taught French and got to know the cook there called Doreen (who had been at the Lycee in Paris) whose son Jonathan was also the same age. The three women and their three little boys spent many jolly holidays together. In those early years they often went to Alderney, to Essex Castle where Lucy Hughes covered as the caretaker. The three little boys were later joined by Jonty Meades from Salisbury and they roamed the island collecting ammunition and letting off bullets and playing with German weaponry, totally ignored by their mothers who were also having a wonderful time, smoking and talking and laughing! They were very happy times. The three little boys all grew up to be very successful. Lucy was a particularly amusing friend and we saw a lot of her over the years. Her son Anthony she called 'The Inkle Pinkle'! She helped Betty Purves at one stage and I remember Jack Purves once saying,

"Where is that blasted Inkle Pinkle?"

In Salisbury Mary Ann had her ex-Army friends and got to know a lot people around and about, but life was very hard and she was continually short of money. Her mother died about this time and her brother, Kenneth told her NOT to come to the funeral. Her mother had left her out of her Will, and Kenneth knew she would make a fuss. She always made a huge fuss when it came to her family and money. These words resonated throughout my childhood,

"My mother hated me, she loved the other two, she cut me out of her Will, the injustice of it, I hate injustice!"

They were well off and thrifty and loved money and talked about money and made money. She had grown up in a rich family and had always taken money for granted and had never saved and never had to and never would! Her siblings were well off with no children and had re-invested their inheritance sensibly! The money that should have been left to her was put in a Trust for the Children, (because she was deemed improvident) and very badly invested and it dwindled! No wonder she always seemed to us to hate 'The Scotch', she meant the Scots as a race, as they were 'mean' and 'dour' 'near' and lived in a cold, wet, dreary place. She hated them all.

She was offered a good job (head of English) at the local convent ' *La Retraite*' in Salisbury right behind her house in Wordsworth Road, and Sarah could have gone to school at the convent free and would be a day girl, they could walk there every day, with George a day boy at Chafyn Grove, round the corner, it was a perfect solution. But Granny Nancy Pelly put a stop to that, she came to see her and made an awful scene because it was a Catholic convent, Granny Pelly was a dyed-in-the-wool Northern Irish Protestant (Orange) and once said that Catholics did not feel pain! She made such a fuss that MA had to give up this idea, so Sarah had to go the Rookesbury Park, a very expensive prep school in Hampshire and MaryAnn had to get herself another better paid job.

So in 1951 she let her house in Salisbury and got a brilliant job at Stokelake School in Chudleigh. Being resident she could make some money. She also got to know her husbands' Irish relations, the Wilson's in Star Cross in Devon as well as the Pellys at Weymouth. The children often spent holidays with their friends. George, who was no problem had been at Chafyn Grove School in Salisbury since he was five and when she went away to work, until the school had room for him as a border, he lived with a family in Salisbury who owned the large drapers shop. George was very happy with them and came home saying 'pardon'.

For two years 1951 – 1953 she worked as Deputy Head at Stokelake School, Chudleigh, Devon, and took over as head when Miss Gribble, the Headmistress was away. It was a lovely little boarding school set in rolling, rural countryside. But she only got full-board for herself, there was no room for her children.

Here is what an ex-pupil I met only recently said of her:

Mary Anne Pelly, as I remember her

Childhood memories are intuitive. We have no experiential context in which to place them so, virtually all experience is new, fresh, unique. Certainly Mary Anne Pelly was unique, even within the context of my limited experience of European customs and people.

The news of her impending arrival at the school, announced by the Headmistress, was appended with the caution that she had been widowed. I took this to mean that we were required to treat her with consideration. It was the early 1950s and many of the students at school had lost their fathers in the 2nd WW, so the fact that Mrs. Pelly was a widow did not come as a surprise. What was a surprise was that she had a degree in history from Cambridge University at a time when women graduates from Oxbridge were few and far between.

So, Mrs. Pelly, as we naturally called her, arrived: slim, loose-limbed in her movements, friendly in her attitude and altogether different, though, at first, it was difficult to say exactly why she stood apart. She already had some grey hairs; she was stylishly dressed, wore make-up and bright nail varnish. She had a husky laugh, smoked and was willing to play tennis with us, though with a curious style that we had not seen before, that is to say, she served under-arm. She explained that in her day, it was not considered lady-like for women to serve the way men do. I do remember that her fore-hand was formidable. It did not take long to realise that she was also a person of strong opinions and had no compunction about airing them.

I should explain that Stokelake School was a small private school situated in South Devon on a hill over-looking the Teign Valley. There were only 40 pupils in the school and, at times, even fewer. It was chosen for my sisters and me by our guardian who felt that in a small school we were likely to receive a greater degree of individual attention which, as non-English speakers, we required in order to catch up with the lessons. The school was started after the 2nd WW by the Headmistress, who had been a teacher (she boasted that she had taught Mary Churchill and was referred to as "Mary's school certificate" by Winston himself!) and the Housekeeper who had met her in the Land Army during the war. The lack of contact with the outside world meant that Stokelake had a kind of rarefied atmosphere. The ethos belonged more to an Edwardian England than the 20th Century post-war era. Of course I only realised this after leaving school. Mary Ann Pelly rocked the boat, for not only did she bring the outside world with her, but also because she consistently questioned what she considered to be out-dated attitudes.

One instance of this was when a group of us decided that we would like to perform a one-act play. Normally we had plays held at the end of the autumn term called "Ships' Plays" (instead of Houses, we had three Ships, called after the ships that fought at the Battle of River Plate: Exeter, Ajax and Achilles) and they took the form of a competition. We had an outside judge who presented the winning play with a trophy. The one act-play was just a venture which we undertook for fun and the advantage was that we could draw on people from different Ships.

We wrote off to French's for one-act plays and had an enormous amount of fun in choosing a really good comedy. Eventually a play entitled "Thirty Minutes in a Street" was chosen by general consensus.

The rehearsals were carried out in strict secrecy in order to surprise the staff and other students with our skills and resourcefulness. Finally the great day arrived and everyone was assembled in the Music Room for the performance. Half way through our performance, and while the students were in fits of laughter, the Headmistress walked out. I felt a slight sense of alarm, but noticed Mrs. Pelly in the front row was literally crying with laughter, which was reassuring.

I remember also how she made a point of remaining behind after the performance and congratulating us on a very imaginative achievement. She did, however, add: "I didn't know you had it in you!" and then left us, still laughing. It appears that, in our innocence, we had chosen a rather risqué play. One of the women in the street was a prostitute and I myself, dressed as a man with a moustache, was a punter! In today's world where children are so "street wise", it seems unimaginable that we simply had no idea who these characters represented. Mrs. Pelly did know but, even so, she was on our side. We needed her protection when we were called before the Headmistress for our misdeeds.

Where I had most contact with Mrs. Pelly was during my English and History classes. There were only two of us taking English A-level, so we had her to ourselves and that was when I began to learn who she really was. It is a lesson that has remained with me, that to know someone well, you need to know their fundamental values regarding life. This is more indicative than any religious or political ideology. Mary Anne Pelly's values were exposed through her literary criticism. She was a realist and hated sentimentality, which I think was part of the reason she did not like Wordsworth. She admired originality and passionately defended freedom of thought. She did her best to encourage me to be adventurous in my writing. She would repeatedly say: "You must un-button yourself". By which I take it she meant I should not be afraid to expose my inner-most thoughts.

As I write this, she comes vividly to mind: her enormous kindness and generosity of spirit. She was remarkably free from prejudice (except perhaps against Wordsworth!). Indeed, she was the first truly tolerant person I had met. I know now, so many years later, that tolerance requires courage and fortitude, qualities which Mary Anne had in abundance.

That was by Gitty Dunham who was from Persia and now lives in Bury St Edmunds

During this period the long holidays continued to be a problem. MA was again homeless. Through the years, Lucy used to invite Doreen and her to Essex Castle where the three boys continued to play with military detritus and weaponry. Every summer Sarah was invited to France.

Bernard

With her Salisbury house let, there were times when there was nowhere to go but Bernard's. Bernard was an old boyfriend from India days. His wife had left him because he was so miserable. He had a very cold cottage in Chute Cadley near Andover and a chicken farm. He loved having Mary Ann to stay because she bought all the food and cooked for him and the children worked on the chicken farm! We hated it! We had to get up early and break ice on the water troughs and lug huge buckets of layers' mash around. We went there repeatedly for a short time because there was nowhere else to go. MA caught Bernard hiding the butter and counting the silver teaspoons!

Happily also Mildred Nicolas used to invite the whole family to Wales where I would go off over the mountains looking for sheep with Tom Nicolas and the sheep dog. Christmas were always with the Pellys at Chickerall. In the summers I would go to France to the Poidatz family and teach them all English and never learned a word of French, whilst George and Mary Ann would go to Scotland to play golf and tour the country with Betty and Jack who then lived in Edinburgh. We always spent some time at Bernard's we knew we had to. There was a lovely pub in the village called The Hatchet run by Nance and Moira who cheered us all up.

Move to Salisbury

In 1954, Mary Ann left Chudleigh where she had been for 2 or 3 years and went for an interview to Salisbury College of Further Education. Most of her old friends were still living in that area. The Langs, the Bens, the Crabtrees had all been at Larkhill when she first came back from India and she had worked at Salisbury Grammar School and at the Convent in the late 40's early 50's. She had a room at Stokelake, but she wanted a proper home. Holidays were a big problem, where to take the children? They were at boarding schools, Sarah at the Royal School, Bath and George at Chafyn Grove in Salisbury and about to go Wellington College.

So she got a very good, very well paid job at Salisbury, as a lecturer teaching English to school leavers and to day-release adults. (Granny Nancy Pelly was waiting in the car during her interview, she says she prayed very hard and God gave her the job!) So she happily sold Wordsworth Road for £3,000 and bought The Green, Upper Woodford for £1800. Who says she was improvident!

The family had often been for drives down the Woodford valley when Mary Ann had taught at The Manor School, Durnford. So we were all thrilled at the thought that we would actually live in Woodford.

The house was in a wonderful position, it was down a rutty lane beside the wide River Avon. Although it was semi-detached, her half of the cottage was on the river side and the neighbour on the inside away from the river. So when we were in the garden we felt totally at one with the river and the withy bed. The old village green was in front and beside the house so it looked really rural. Water was from a well via an electric pump but was later connected to the mains. There was a small coke-burning Aga-type stove in the kitchen which kept it nice and warm and heated the water. It had been completely done up by a builder and was very clean and spruce. It was called The Green, in Upper Woodford 8 miles from Salisbury, so Mary Ann had to have a car. These two little cottages had a wonderful outlook up the valley over the water-meadows towards Durnford. There were walks up the valley and along the river to Durn-ford. The road on the other side of the river was a dead-end so there was little traffic. Although it was beside the river it was a very old site and never flooded. The water would come nearly all round the house but never into it!

Upper Woodford was the largest village in the valley. It had a pub, The Bridge Inn, a blacksmith, a garage where Mr Target mended her cars, a Post Office and a wonderful village shop called The Home Market which was a grocer and a butcher where Mrs Pelly naturally had an account!

At the College of Further Education MA taught trainee-nurses and secretarial students whom she loved and young mechanics whom she loathed. These were ex-secondary-modern teenagers who had to pass 'O' level English in order to work in a garage or shop and had to know how to write invoices. The mechanics day- release used to play her up like mad. She felt they were totally out of control, drawing bosomy women on the black-board the moment her back was turned. Her boss Mr.Oates, gave her all sorts of hints, like pretending to write their names in a little black book. The worst one was called Benstead who lived in our village, if we drove past him he would bow! He was known as 'Bedstead'. One day when they were particularly riotous, she hit one as hard as she could on the side of the head with a book! She later moved to the Commerce Department which she loved.

In contrast, she adored the young women and girls. They were trainee-nurses and clerks or secretaries who all knew her in later life and would greet her in the street. I once came across an English lesson (because my school holidays overlapped), situated outside on the lawn at the end of the summer term, in the shade of a tree, when the girls, sitting on the grass were reading a Shakespeare play aloud, as I approached I was told,

'Ssshh! Mrs. Pelly is sleeping!' When I confronted her later she admitted to the tedium of listening to broad Wiltshire in blank verse! They adored reading Shakespeare round the class.

She made a lot of friends at the 'Tec' as we called it, a woman who taught dressmaking helped her to make some curtains, but said she had to practice in the lunch hour on newspaper because the treadle sewing-machine ran away with her!

Although her degree was in History she taught O-level and A-level English with such success that when she retired in 1966 she was re-hired by the Salisbury College for Further Education twice to get the teenagers through their exams and continued working until she was 70, she loved it. She had worked very hard, most evenings she came home with huge piles of books to correct. She told us that she sometimes woke up at 2am in the morning surrounded by corrections. To make money she also used to mark exam papers from outside sources in the holidays. At one stage she was paying super tax because she had her pay and her pension! But it was soon sorted out.

The Neighbours

Mary Ann never got on with her immediate neighbours! In 1955 Mr. P a Scot, next door told her that all the land round about her house was his. He called it his 'estate' and he used to fill it in with great lorry loads of earth. He worked for the council Roads Department. She did not take him too seriously, but he was very abrupt and morose. As a teenager I took him very seriously and hated him. He had a down-trodden wife and a privy at the bottom of the garden. From our bathroom window we would see him coming up the garden path each morning, buttoning up his flies.

He said he owned all the land round our cottage and had also bought the strip between our garden and the river. As a family we felt totally dominated by him, at least I did. He used our garage which was very large with its back to the river and he would reverse Mary Ann's car out for her every morning.

He was kind in some ways. My mother had to pay him through the nose to get our garden extended to the river. Also later to buy small sections he said were his. I think my mother had a very bad solicitor when she originally bought the property.

We used to worry about Mr. P and his 'estate' as he called it. He was horrid to his wife who was very kind to my brother George who would go round to watch their telly. When she died and I said I was sorry, all he could say was,

"Now we have to make our own tea and all!"

As soon as she died he put in a proper bathroom and loo and built on a lovely sun room which she would have loved. (I suspect he had some sort of life insurance on his wife.) Mr. P was our ogre and we used to laugh at him and fear him. A member of the parish council alerted my mother to an application for planning permission from them for a house on the village green.

In the end MA managed to buy bits of land back from him, it was the ancient village green. The village had moved and ours was the only house left. Being on the spit of land which never gets flooded, in winter sometimes the swans swim up to the back door!

In the summer holiday of 1957 Mr. P organised jobs for my brother and me counting cars for surveys on the traffic round Stonehenge where they still have not put a bypass! He probably wanted to help the poor widow next door.

When he died, our next neighbour made us appreciate Mr. P's good points. She was Mrs C who thought she was very grand and objected violently to my mother's washing. So she put up a huge fence between our gardens. The previous one had been a few poles with roses climbing up and through them and hardly seemed a dividing line. She objected to the dog, the cars, the noise and always with a solicitor's letter. When she sold up, Babs an old friend suggested that she bought the house and told George she would leave it to him. Then as so often with Babs she changed her mind. Poor George. Then the B's bought the house and were there for 30 years. George had his eye on the house and has bought it. Now The Green is three times its original size and quite lovely, but sometimes being lonely down there a neighbour would be quite useful.

Growing up

We had a very happy childhood at The Green. I went there when I was about 14 and George 11. Some Sundays we'd go to church to meet other people in the valley. We were quite pretentious. M A used to beg us not to go, so we could help her get Sunday lunch, but no, we went to church sometimes just to annoy her.

She never ever went to church. She said that there was no God.

"How could there be when he had killed my father in the First World War and my husband in the Second!"

We used to bicycle into Salisbury on Sunday evenings to watch 'b' movies. We would see two, then bicycle home again. Eight miles each way. The road was through woods beside the river and I remember being terrified having watched Dracula and seeing bats swooping down in front of me.

MA was a wonderfully vague mother. She was very thin and George and I were both very fat. Everyone used to point out how fat we were and how skinny she was! So she took us to a dietician in London. He looked at us all and said she should have malt every day and complan. He thought we were very fine specimens! After the war everyone else was so thin.

Robin

In 1958 make a bit more money we had Robin Paterson to stay in the holidays. He was about 14 or 15 and a border at Millfield School. His parents were divorced and one lived in Bahamas and the other in Kenya. We only had a black and white telly which snowed most of the time. We used to play cards for money. Canasta, Poker, Hearts, and Gin Rummy. We fleeced Robin and he fleeced us back. We had great fun with him. He was very nice and loved Mary Ann. He visited her years later and told her how happy he had been.

She was quite vague about what we were up to. George was always very placid and good and I was not. She was also very generous, I was always fishing in her bag for 'small change' (half-crowns 2/6) and she used it say 'it's ours'. George had been to Chafyn Grove the local school and had lots of friends and was very popular with the girls. He was always being invited to dances. He had been to Miss Pinniger's dancing lessons, he did 'the forward side together, back side together', Waltz, the gay Gordons, Eightsomes etc. Our mother was furious one evening when he refused an invitation to a hunt ball and said that someone else had also invited him and had paid for his ticket too. George has always been very canny with money and later very successful too.

George stayed with our mother long after I had left home. She did not want the bore of having to ferry him everywhere so he cashed his Post Office savings and bought himself a small (phut phut) motor bike which was always falling to pieces (because he was so heavy!). He joined the Army and bought a car and was based nearby so he would often pop in to see her and stay whenever he wanted. He lived a very jolly life with plenty of girlfriends.

MaryAnn's friends were legion. There was always the bridge contingent.

Also there were three or four widows, well one never heard about their husbands, but there was usually one offspring. Like Doreen and Lucy, great girls who during the war had been 'let down' so were widows like my mother. They all had little boys the same age and would spend holidays *together* and a lot of fun. They were usually cooks in schools, so they had the school holidays and lived-in enjoying excellent living arrangements and sometimes almost free education. Their children have all done very well and risen to the top of their professions owing no doubt to the fact that it was up to them to make the most of life.

There were dozens of relations and hangers-on. People were always coming to stay sometimes for months at a time. She would laugh about them.

"Well I told her it was time for them to buy the next bottle of gin!"

The village shop was very protective of her. One weekend when she was away, Bernard's new wife N., ordered a leg of lamb and they refused to put it on her account! They were mortified and embarrassed. But it had been me who had alerted the village shop and of course they loved the chance to help out and have a bit of gossip.

George had failed the civil service exam into the army from Wellington College and our mother told him to join up (instead of going to a Crammer). After a few months as the Quantity Surveyor trainee, he did join up and he was only 6 months behind his fellow recruits at Sandhurst.

Chapter 6

MARY ANN AND CARS

'The sickening screech of tearing metal' quote (MA)
1934 India killed cow
1956 High Post
1969 Weymouth
1970 Lake
1976 Royston on the way to Sarah
1981 Salisbury

MY MOTHER REALLY enjoyed her life and had masses of friends. She lived it to the full. She loved her children and loved her job teaching in Salisbury which was 8 miles from home. It was a very good job and she was very well paid. She was much respected at the College and she got very good results. She worked extremely hard living alone during term time. We were both away at school but would catch her doing corrections till 3 am when our holidays overlapped with her term times.

Mary Ann was a terrible driver, she had never taken a test and even after she lost her license for a year through dangerous driving, she was not re-tested! If a lorry tried to pass her, her foot would automatically go down onto the accelerator, even in very old age. It was the competitive streak, she liked to win and she always wanted to be the best in the things that were important to her. The fact that a lorry was passing her was more than she could bear, until it was pointed out that she had to go slowly just for a week or two to run-in her beautiful new car!

She smoked all the time but did not inhale and it did not smell. She just puffed away and the ash and the tip of her cigarettes often fell into her lap burning a hole in her coat, skirt and her petticoat. The driving seat sometimes had a burn hole in it.

In fact her house and mine are littered with black holes from her cigarettes. Once or twice she claimed on the insurance for a ruined coat.

MA loved playing Bridge. She played at least once a week. She was quite good and very quick. She played a lot with her friends and at the Bridge Club, she was fun and competitive, but she did not follow the rules all the time. She played for money, small stakes and never minded how much she lost. Most of her bridge was played privately with supper and until late at night. Usually she went home to walk the dog after work, but sometimes she would have tea in town. Then later would drive to friends to play bridge and have supper. So sometimes it was very late when she went home to The Green. She had many hairy encounters at that time of night.

It was in 1957 that she lost her license. She had never passed a test but in 1947 she did not need one. She had to have a car to get to work. She was always an incompetent driver. To start, she used to roar the engine and lean forward and make a pushing motion as though on a horse. She discovered that changing gear was not always necessary if she roared the engine enough and feathered the clutch. She was proud of the fact that she always gave bicycles lots of space, and that she really respected cyclists.

She spent a lot of money on her cars, she usually had a new second-hand ones. The first I remember was a little square Ford with bright blue wheels which would not go up the hill at Dartmouth with George and me in it because we were so fat and heavy. She then had a Hillman Minx which she loved, then a Consul which she could not control and used to go round corners on two wheels. After that she got an 1100, then Triumph Heralds, they were very popular smart, small and cheap. It was in this car that she lost her license.

1955, Sarah, Brigitte Poidatz. Ann Purves behind Anthony, George and Jonathan the three little boys. The Hillman Minx with the old garage.

She usually went into Salisbury along the valley road which was winding and pretty, but sometimes she would go in via High Post up on the 'Down' which was the main road from Amesbury to Salisbury A 30, this was the quickest. You could see the traffic coming in both directions. This particular day she was late. She saw a double-decker bus coming very slowly up the rise towards Salisbury with a long queue of cars behind it. She roared the engine, let out the clutch and lurched in front of the bus and tootled off delightedly to college. The bus had to pull up and a concertina of crashed cars built up behind it. The police visited her at College later and she went to court and was banned from driving for a year.

As she needed to drive to get to work, she let the house and moved into Salisbury for a year and may have enjoyed a different sort of life. I can't remember what we all did being away at school most of the time. I expect we went to friends for the holidays.

One night she was going along the Salisbury /Amesbury road late, when a soldier stepped out into the middle of the road in front of her. She could not avoid him and he was hit hard and went up over the top of the car to land behind her. She was terrified and stopped and went to him. She sat at the side of the road with his head cradled in her lap until a passing motorist telephoned the ambulance. When it came they took him off to hospital told her to go home as there nothing she could do, although she offered go with him. She awoke early and in great trepidation phoned but could get no response from the hospital until later in the morning. She phoned again in the lunch hour to ask about the 'hit' victim who had been brought in during the night. They said that he was still drunk but had discharged himself and had left!

One of her great friends was Bunty Meades, (Mother to Jonathan T Meades). After bridge with her in Harnham, a suburb south of Salisbury my mother would drive home via Wilton which saved going back through the town. The turning from Wilton was on the right but a large new roundabout had been built at the junction. So at two one morning she arrived at the roundabout and turned sharp right cutting out the rest of the roundabout. A policeman stepped out in front of her with a torch and asked her what she thought she was doing. She upbraided him scornfully,

'Don't be so stupid. At this time of night, of course I am not going to go all the way round the roundabout when I just need to go right!'

'A safe journey to you Madam,' was all he said.

Going to stay with our dear Pelly relations at Chickerall near Weymouth Mary Ann hit another car going round a big bend on the hill above Weymouth. She stayed down there with them and returned by train. I borrowed another car from Viv and Jess Seivewright actually also a Triumph Herald to take her down to collect her car so that it could be repaired by her local garage Mr. Target. On the way back I was following her and saw her overtake a car which had indicated it was turning right and she passed it on the right and of course it went straight into her. She swore she had not seen it indicating and I could not defend her. But she was totally unfazed by the incident and said the Insurance would pay, and they did. If they refused she would change companies.

'I have done a terrible thing!' She said on the phone one day, she was always saying it about all sorts of incidents and my heart sank, she lived in Wiltshire and I in Suffolk. This time it was hitting an oil tanker on the valley road in Lake.

'I was going much too fast,' she said. It was a trip to London to stay with Babs and go to the theatre. Her car rolled onto its roof it was a red Morris 1100 and she crawled out of the window with only a cut finger. Her friends, the Alexanders who lived in the village came across her and seeing she was alright drove on, Jack, the husband did not want to miss the first race at Newbury, so seeing she was OK left her to it! She was very hurt and wondered if she could ever speak to them again. She did of course and they remained some of her best friends. She got the train to London and had a lovely weekend with Babs and had to get a new car. It was a Peugeot, pale blue.

In 1958 I was learning to drive, and had a few lessons but needed practice.

'You drive beautifully', my mother said, 'Be careful of cows, but take the car when you want'. (I found out later that when she was driving in India she had killed a cow and there had been a terrible fuss, she had had to go to the temple with offerings!) It was a bore for her to take me to the tennis club after work so I just drove myself without L plates on the car. When the time came to take my test I drove up in the car to the test centre and of course they refused to let me take the test and hauled my mother over the coals. She was old and tired and fed up with me.

I took it in London the next year when I was a student staying with Babs and I remember the man came to take me for my test and I was lying on my bed still in the dance dress and earrings from the night before, I was too hung over to do anything wrong so passed first go. It was the day Princess Margaret got married.

The great thing about MA was that she laughed and laughed at herself. The funniest things happened. She was sitting at home with her respectable friends playing bridge one afternoon when a police car drew up and the policeman said he had come to arrest her for car theft. She went out with them and they looked at her Triumph Herald which was almost new. But it was not hers, she had driven off in an identical car which was owned by an irate member of staff at the College. How they all laughed!

Ultimately she killed someone. Babs was one of my mother's oldest friends and they had known each other as children in Edinburgh during the Great War. She was one of the many spinsters of that ilk when all the young men had been killed and there was no one left for them to marry. After many happy years as friends Mary Ann sadly admitted that she killed Babs in her last car crash. Babs was staying with her recouping from a broken hip. They were going to the theatre in Salisbury and driving along the Devizes Road high up above Salisbury and Babs asked what the lights were, M A turned her head and whole body to look and crashed into the lamp post. She broke her leg, ankle, arm and wrist. Her hip came out of its socket and was never put back and Babs broke her pelvis and never really recovered.

Mary Ann recovered but could never drive again and lived another ten years but Babs died that year having been taken to live with friends at Lymington to whom she had promised to leave everything. – Quite a fortune!

The Devizes Road bears testament to MA's driving, the lamp-posts are all concrete except one, which is metal, it looks like a slim wand compared to the other stout, substantial ones! She was sent the bill for it!

After the accident she and Babs went to a very nice nursing home and one day when I visited her the nurses were all laughing. 'Your mother disappeared', they said. It seems she was sitting in the bath which had a large mirror on the cupboard door beside it. She got confused by the reflection in the mirror of the room behind her. Stood up pulling on the door which opened and she climbed inside the cupboard. The nurses could not understand where she had gone. They found her sitting in the cupboard amongst the towels, warm and cosy. When I visited her there always seemed to be something to smile about.

Babs and M A had climbed a lot in the Alps when they were young between the Wars and had had many holidays together. She became blind and stayed with MA before going to her friends in Lymington.

Chapter 7

THE GREEN 1955 – 70'S

MARY ANN BOUGHT The Green, Upper Woodford in 1955 for £1800. It was tucked away down a muddy lane beside the ancient village green. The house was semi-detached with a large garage backing on to the River Avon. A little bit of withy bed separated the house from the river. She never had fishing rights but asked Lady Janet Bailey the landowner, if I could fish. So we were allowed to fish for grayling which meant that we could not fish during the summer. But I used to fish when nobody was around and was always being caught by the water bailiff, Mr Green. However I would invite him in for a beer and he would forgive me and I would show him the letter from Lady Janet. I did not disturb the fishermen who paid. There were many, and they would park their cars beside our house. One, Mr. Whiting, taught me to fish, his wife did not like gutting trout so he would give them to Mary Ann. She always called him Mr Grayling which was most embarrassing. "Mr Grayling come in out of the rain and have a whisky!"

River Avon

1954, withy bed and river

Mary Ann in garden next to whithy bed, with river behind.

We had a wonderful woman called Mrs Olive Feltham who came in to the house to clean almost every other day. She would arrive at about 9.00 with a great "Halloo". In later years' she would settle down to have breakfast with my mother. Her husband Alec had been in the war, a Sergeant in the Black Watch he had been at Dunkirk and then all through Italy. He worked for the Bailey estate and they had a tithe cottage in the village. He was a sweet man and would help out when needed. He would meet us all at the station when coming down from London after MA stopped driving.

In 1957 Jack and Gwen Alexander moved into the village, they had a large house beside the pub and some fishing opposite. When we first met them a mutual friend told them that Sarah would take him fishing! Jack had been Secretary to the Sultan of Zanzibar and was a very dignified old gent. He was mortified when accosted by Mr Green the water bailiff, and many apologies ensued!

My mother's cottage always seemed full of people. There were the Purves cousins, Betty's in laws. The mother, Georgie Purves was a very good artist and the children very bright. Their daughter Ann Purves was at the Royal School with me and went on to Cambridge. She came to France with Brigitte and me after Brigitte had been staying with us. Ann at 17 was very opinionated and the Poidatz's found her rather rude. Ann married very young and sadly died aged only about 30 of MS leaving 3 children.

In 1959 I was given a springer spaniel puppy called Gilly which I naturally brought home to MA. A couple of months later I went up to London to do Speech Therapy with never a backward glance I left her with my mother and F., she was a dear dog a great success.

The cottage was very popular with our friends, people would pile in, and I always opted to sleep in the kitchen. It was beautiful in the summer, we as children would go to Durnford to play cricket on the village green. Then walk back along past the Mill where Aylmer Tryon lived, we could swim there diving into the deep mill pond and be swept into the shallows.

Mrs Feltham, aka 'F' knew everybody in the valley and most of what went on too. Her great friend was Mrs Chitty who 'did' for Aylmer Tryon up at the Mill at Durnford. The Tryons owned Durnford Manor School. Lord Tryon was 'Keeper of the Privy Purse'. They were very grand and were in with the Royal family, Prince Charles used to be a frequent visitor to 'Kanga' Tryon. Aylmer owned a gallery in London and had retired to Durnford. One day there was great excitement because the Queen Mother who was on a visit was coming to tea with Aylmer. Mrs F was full of it. Now, Mrs Chitty certainly had one up on her, talk about cleaning, she had been polishing for weeks! And Mrs Chitty was going to serve the tea too. Well the great day came and when it came to pouring out the tea, it was purple! How the Queen Mum laughed. Mrs Chitty had left a Brillo Pad in the teapot!

In the early 60's during term time F always took the dog home with her, it was a very short walk. Her house was along the main (B) road from our turning and the dog would wait outside for MA to sound her horn and run down beside the car, there was very little traffic in those days.

We had many lovely holidays with our mother. She took us to Dartmouth one year with the Meades family, where she borrowed the Purves's house on Mount Boom opposite the Dartmouth Naval College. We took Brigitte Poidatz who was over having an exchange with us. She loved England and practiced English all the time.

We were quite poor, but if MA had any spare cash she would spend it on a holiday. Aunt Kitty came to our rescue in this regard. Her cheques would come winging onto her desk when most needed. In summer 1955 we went to Brittany to St Brieuc with Lucy and Anthony.

Then in 1957 Mary Ann drove us out to Switzerland. Babs, her great climbing friend from her youth was a member of the Scottish Woman's Alpine Club and arranged for us as a family to borrow their mountain hut in St Luc. It was called the 'Laiterie', hay above; cows below, only there we no cows as they were up on the pasture. MA organised that we should climb a real mountain. She hired a guide called Maurice and he took us up to a mountaineers' cabin where we stayed the night with many other climbers and rose at 3 a.m. so that we could climb the 'Besso' before the clouds arrived. MA could not climb, she had had a broken ankle and could not balance on the moraine, but she came to the hut. Then she waited till we had climbed the peak. The three of us climbed lots of little peaks all round St Luc and had a wonderful holiday, once again thanks to Aunt Kitty!

MA's 90th Birthday with all the Pellys

1990, MA feeding the pheasant. Ten years with her pronged stick.

1970 – 1992 Playing bridge with Betty Hall and friends.

MA, Jane Pelly (Mills), Nancy (Lady Clark) , Sally (Lady Morony), Sarah at The Elms summer 1985.

The front with garage extension, 1990

Back with old sunroom MA's bedroom, 1990

Chapter 8

My MOTHER WAS a member of the Golf Club, her first round there was memorable. She had last played in India in Gulmarg, so was out of practice with everything. That first day, when she came in she found she had lost most of her clubs! The people coming in behind her had them! She had been in the habit of throwing them on the ground expecting her Indian Caddy to pick them up! She soon learned! She loved golf and we all joined High Post Golf Club. It was a very important part of her life and she had many friends there.

The members, mostly 'Army' were interested in her family and our life in general. 'What are the children doing now?' She was asked, 'Sarah is a bar maid and George is a Private!' Was the answer. There was a very nice old General living in Colts Corner, a house at the top of our lane, and he used to play golf with George.

Someone said to George, "Don't you think you should call Jim 'Sir', after all he is a General and you are a Private!" We were very spoilt!

MA's garden at The Green was also very pretty with the River Avon running along one side. Her great love was the weeping ornamental cherry, in the spring it was like a huge white fountain in the middle of the garden. She would say,

"The only thing I have done with my life are Sarah and George and the Cherry Tree", she would sit in its shade in the summer. The lawn went right down to the river where there was a bench she would sit on in the evenings. Over the years Fishers (Piscatorial Society) would slowly walk past and we were always very careful not to disturb them. They paid huge sums to fish for trout.

There were some interesting people living in the Woodford Valley, Lady Janet Bailey, daughter of the Earl of Inchcape was married to a relation of our present neighbour Julia Budworth who was a Bailey, and a Mitford. I am not sure of the connection. Clementine Calver Nee Bailey was married to a vet called Peter Calver whose horse *Highland Wedding* won the Grand National. They lived at the end of the lane in Colt's Corner the nice house owned by Lady Janet. They had a little meadow next door, beside Mrs Appleby's cottage with two loose boxes in it. Well one winter's day Lady Janet payed them a surprise visit and because it was very cold and the looseboxes were draughty and because one of the horses was ill, Lady Janet found the horse in the sitting room of Colt's Corner! It seemed quite natural to Clementine that since it needed close attention it could come in the house! I had got to know them quite well as I used to ride out early in the morning with them both. The horse I rode was a hack called Granite who loved watching aeroplanes circling, which was quite un-nerving as there were lots of planes from RAF Boscombe Down nearby. After Lady Janet found the horse in her sitting room the Calvers moved!

In the early days 1956 Mrs Appleby had an Arab stallion called Hussein and she taught riding at Durnford Manor School. The children at the school were all borders and they brought their own ponies from home with them to school. Those were the days!

Lady Janet Bailey's house in Lake has been owned by Sting for the last 20 years!

MA had a gardener called Derek who worked for the Tryons and he used to bring in dahlias and chrysanthemums left over from their borders. He was a very kind man who was a widower and had a difficult son, always in trouble. He came twice a month and mowed the lawn and always stayed for a chat. When she was lame and could not drive he would do all her shopping for her at the supermarket in Salisbury. He was so helpful and always stayed for a drink afterwards. He liked whisky.

Mary Ann was a real character and said some of the funniest things!

As mentioned previously MA smoked a lot, so did both children, but I tried to give up with a friend. This episode happened in Mauritius, when she came to stay there with us. The friend, Jean Gardner was quite religious and said she prayed to God to help her to give up smoking. One day we had all been out together and had had a bit of a fracas and lost the children and we all came in to the house rather upset. On this day she was with us and my mother offered her a cigarette as she was about to light up herself.

"Oh No! Jesus told me not to!" says religious Jean. Well my mother had never heard anybody speak like that before and thought she must have a husband called Jason who had told her not to.

"Well! I don't suppose he smokes" says Mary Ann.

My friend gave my mother a very odd look.

Back in Wiltshire talking to her friends they had heard her ranting as usual about television and how there was nothing one wanted to watch on it.

She said, "I came in the other night late and put it on to see the news, all there was, was a couple um, you know what is the polite word for *Fuck*".

Laughter.

"Sexual intercourse Mary Ann!"

One day I rang her and she said she could not possibly talk, she was watching football, it was the World Cup.

After her last car crash, and recuperation, she went home with Gwen a very good friend of Betty's who came down from Newcastle.

November 5th 1981 to Sarah in Saudi Arabia.

Darling Sarah,

Such a lovely letter you sound terribly busy and happy, it must be fun having Susie (Willings) back for a bit. 18 to dinner my mind boggles, luckily you've boys to wash up and prepare the veg. No doubt you do the cooking and sweets ugh!

Well darling, things are not so bright & beamish having Babs here. You know she had the shock treatment and has now bought her flat – but she is not even 50%, and God knows what will happen when she lives alone? She's half blind and very tottery, it's her bad feet, she says, nothing to do with the accident but she's got so greedy and aggressive. Also she wants 100 wat bulbs everywhere, as she says she can't see. I have to cook far more food than we ever had, or with Gwen and she's still so thin I feel she must need it, but she eats far more than George and I find it such a bind preparing meals as I'm so slow. She said she would cook left over chicken and rice one evening and she covered with kitchen floor with chicken and mess and it was dead cold. She said she didn't realize she had to heat the chicken in the rice. She can't see prop-erly – so makes such a mess everywhere. Her breakfast is a marathon and takes about an hour. I just have my bath and leave her and poor F usually cleans up the mess.

Lovely weather, I had lunch in the garden, I miss Gwen a lot Babs is a very poor substitute. She's gone up to London today, but only for one night to some religious group. I asked if she's get a good meal – it's at a friend's house but only tea and biscuits. So she's staying at her club in Albemarle St. and back p.m. tomorrow, Alec is meeting her.

Betty Hall brought 3 out last Sunday for bridge and again next Sunday and we see Gwen Alexander & Nancy who takes us shopping. Gwen is very worried about Jack who isn't at all well and getting slower than me. So sad old age.

F & Alec are marvellous and make life quite easy. So much love and to Jonathan.

Ps Glad you're teaching drama, up your street.

I make all my cakes like Juliet's and so does F. Success.

She carried on as though nothing had changed. She made beautiful cakes.

She had a three-pronged stick which stood alone. Her shoe was built up three inches. She learned to cook using minimum ingredients. Eg: 1 packet dried onion soup, 4 pork chops, packet of Uncle Ben's rice.

People came to stay in their droves, she loved it and they took her about in their cars and she carried on life as usual. She was often lonely and would ring me up complaining about what Mr Wilson (the Prime Minister) had said! George and I were married and had children so could not stay with her much. But the faithful F (now a widow) would come regularly, 3 or 4 times a week. Her bridge players all came to supper regularly usually on a Saturday, as telly was awful on a Saturday. They came in 3's!

Although she loved me I knew she must have been very disappointed that I was not an intellectual success. She would say, 'You can't concentrate on anything for more than 5 minutes at a time! All those years at school and you learned nothing.'

'You're quite right although I can chop up an onion perfectly', I'd reply,

'All those summers in France, and you learned nothing!'

'I leaned not to cut the nose off the cheese! And I taught them English!'

'But you are a great success my darling' she would say, 'look at your beautiful, clever children!' She was always so positive and so right.

London 1982-96. Jonathan was working for RTZ now Rio Tinto

I could never see enough of my mother and after a weekend with her I would sometimes bring her back to London, if Jonathan was away in Africa, which he was a lot of the time. It would have to be arranged in advance as she had so many commitments in Woodford. But I would drive her up early on a Monday morning, after a weekend there and have a few days in London and then take her back midweek.

She loved our flat in London. It had huge windows looking onto Nightingale Lane, with so much going on. (Very different from her outlook at the cottage in the winter which was a muddy lane and lawn and rabbits and birds.) She sat by the huge sash window and watched children going to school first thing, then the old people from the Home for Aged Jews, and the other Home for Aged Gentiles as she called it, they would be going up and down in their carriages and scooters.

Also her great friend Jennifer aged 80 and still working part-time would often come and spend the day. It was lovely to hear the echo of all the old friends saying 'Mary Ann do you remember in India....?

I would invite a teacher from the school for the deaf where I was working just across the road, like Deidre or Hildi, to come for lunch or tea, so she would have a lot of visitors.

Berry and Audrey, Aunt Kitty's son and daughter in law came for lunch which was great fun, they lived in a basement and loved our lovely airy light flat and loved seeing M A again.

Jonathan's favourite cousin Rosemary asked if she could come to stay. I said of course she must come we had a spare room and my mother and I would share a bed. Oh No she would sleep on the floor. But we said absolutely No, Mother and I would share our bed, it was huge and had a bathroom right next to it for my mother. We had a very jolly evening and she said she had heard my mother on the radio with Jonathan's sister Veronica and we all had a good laugh about how she only wanted to have fun, was not interested in politics or being a suffragette also she had known Rosemary's mother Muriel Lowis in India and had played tennis with her in Peshawar, and we children were the same age and had shared a dooli (a bit like a sedan chair, 2 Indians would carry 2 babies in it, we sat there like lords). So it was lovely to see her. Rosemary was very poor and wanted to buy us a bottle of wine at the local deli but we would not allow it. (Rosemary's father Muriel's husband John had died and she gave the contents of their large house to Oxfam before going into a Home). She did not offer Rosemary anything.

So we made sure she was really comfortable in our nice spare room and Mum and I got into bed together. Well although it was a huge bed, with one thing and another, she kept talking not to mention the snoring and got up in the night. The morning could not come soon enough. I told her not to let on about our disruptive night.

At breakfast when asked how she slept, she said vehemently that had never had such a ghastly night!

I had to get off to work and when I got back I found Rosemary had been out and bought 2 bottles of wine!

Chapter 9

MA's Friends

Chris Royle

CHRISTABEL KNOWN AS Chris Royle (ne Forbes Dalrymple) was a friend of my mother's from childhood and in 1935 had shared a houseboat with her in Kashmir. She was renowned, she had shot her lover on 'Pindi station! (Rawalpindi) I never got to the bottom on that story it was very long and convoluted. She was one of her oldest friends, terribly generous, with wonderful taste but impractical and woefully impecunious.

We were going to visit her in her council house in Street, Somerset. I was staying with my mother for the weekend and noted that we had a sack of coal and a sack of logs in the boot of the Morris 1100. On the back seat was a box with a bottle of whisky, a bottle of gin, bottle of sherry, bottle of vermouth two bottles of wine and a few lemons and books in it.

"Why are you taking so much?" I asked. We were only going for lunch.

"Chris is so generous and so *poor*", was the reply. It was no good arguing with my mother, she was known to have given the coat off her back.

"She lives in a council house," my mother explained, 'she had to sell her lovely house to buy her son a lorry!"

Her son it seemed was furious that she had broken a Trust Fund left to him by his father who had been killed in the war. She had bought houses with it and done them up beautifully, and lost money on every one of them!

"Because she is a fool!" My mother explained, "But she's educated," I interjected, "Look at all the French literature you are taking her!"

Chris it seems had inherited a very large estate in the Highlands with a good many farms on it at the age of about 18 in about 1915. She was the eldest of three children 2 girls and a boy. Both parents had died. She was highly educated and had been to the Sorbonne. Her solicitor was one of my mother's uncles and that is how they knew each other from childhood in Scotland. Chris was sole executor of the Will and she just went through it. No one knows the details.

But every time one of them needed anything she would sell a farm. But one can imagine why her son was so angry.

"Anyway he is horrid," said my mother.

We arrived at the council house where Chris lived. It was winter and cold, wet and windy with wet paths and back doors and rows of tin dishes outside. I remember in the past she had always had nice houses with lots of springer-spaniels. It turned out that she had no dogs. The Council had taken them away from her, because of her indebtedness.

"These people don't feed their dogs properly", said Chris. She had been feeding all the neighbours' dogs and of course they were furious!

In the good old days, in my twenties I had driven down and had stayed with Chris. She had a nice house (an old rectory) and a pack of springers. We had one of hers, she was such a good friend of ours and she had been sweet. She did not drive and I took her to a little pub she knew of with a fruit machine. My mother had warned me that she had no money so I was rather horrified that she played on the fruit machine for some time. I am rather bossy, and I told her to stop. She stopped immediately. A large man came along who must have been watching her, and first go he got the jackpot. She never said a word. She was so nice. I felt awful.

Anyway here we were in this miserable little semi-detached council house and we settled down to stiff martinis and she smoked *Gaitanis*. It was fun, she was thrilled with the company. Lunch in her tiny sitting-room/diner with huge portraits of horses and men stacked along the damp looking walls, was Sole Veronique followed by Partridges all beautifully cooked. There was lots of laughter, and deep discussion, she was very well informed.

"Now you see," said Mary Ann, "why she won't let me take her out to lunch!"

"Restaurant food is so ghastly", said Chris.

The conversation was very lively all about Afghanistan and the government and politics.

I remember the last time I had seen her, we had taken her out to lunch, it was in a grand crowded restaurant and the food had been disappointing, and she told us of a niece of hers who was trying to divorce her very loving husband for the second time. We (my mother and I) said it was very unlikely that she would get a divorce for the second time. Even though he had interfered with her sons. Chris who was talking very loudly said,'

"She has every reason to divorce him, INCEST and BUGGERY!"

The hubbub of the dining room was silenced.

95

Chris was a very ordinary looking woman who could have been a house-keeper.

Here she was in this miserable damp council house, money all gone, a son and daughter- in-law who rightly blamed her for taking all their inheritance, and no dog!

Before we left, Chris pulled out a huge portfolio of her brother's sketches and paintings and told us to choose some to have. They were really lovely he had never married and had lived in Antibes in the South of France all his life and was quite a famous painter by the name of Forbes Dalrymple, Chris' maiden name.

I chose two or three lovely paintings.

Now I could see now why the car had been full of sacks of coal and whisky!

I wished I had bought her a bottle of brandy!

Fat D another of MA's friends

One has friends for all sorts of reasons usually because one has known them for so long, not that one admires them or even likes them!

Fat D was one of these.

MA had known her since they met at Wimbledon playing tennis, in 1920. D was a very good player, my mother not quite as good.

D came from a well healed family who owned the Branksome Towers Hotel in Bournemouth. A paradise to grow up in with enormous grounds and a beach. They met playing in tennis tournaments around the country and on the continent. So when she went to India in 1934, MA looked up Dorothy and her husband Pip, (according to Jennifer, a 'ranker') continuing the friendship in Peshawar. When she eventually returned to Salisbury, England after the war MA looked up D who was living in Bournemouth with a very nice new husband whom everybody adored. Their tennis days were over but they used to see each other regularly, more than M A really wanted and less then D hoped for. When her husband became old and ill D went on a pre-planned holiday and told her daughter, 'I don't want my holiday interrupted. If he dies when I am away, have him put in a freezer until I return!'

Later on when MA was one of her very few friends she would say 'When can I come and spend the day with you and have some bridge?' MA would say 'Well who can I ask to play with you? Last time you threw your cards face up on the table, Joe and Annie won't play with you ever again!' She would say 'Oh well, try someone else!'

D had a long suffering daughter called Shirley who we knew very well, and we would always laugh about D who had a lovely bungalow and covered the floor with newspapers in case we brought in any mud!

Babs

MA had known Babs since childhood in Edinburgh. They were the same age born round the turn of the century and therefore, as young adults had had few boyfriends, as they had all been killed in The Great War. Babs' real name was Griselda Paterson and she worked for the BBC in London and produced Woman's Hour before the War. She was a tall strong good-looking woman, like Mary Ann a climber and belonged to the Woman's Alpine Club and lived in Finchley. They were very good friends and went to exhibitions and theatres together. She was extremely intellectual, cultured and very interested in what my mother called 'isms'. Budism etc., which MA could not be bothered with. When she left the BBC she worked as a Drama teacher at a school in Highgate and for Charity. She produced plays at Wormwood Scrubs prison. I lodged with her for a year when I first went to London to do Speech Therapy. She took me with her to Wormwood scrubs to watch her producing the current play. The lead in the play was a 'Trusty' called Emit Dunn, a famous murderer, who had killed his neighbour and married the neighbour's wife. He got away with it for five years, until they sent a Christmas card to another ex-neighbour who reopened the case! Emit was so honest, Babs used to take packets of cigarettes and hide them about the place for the inmates to find. Before she left Emit would present them to her. Cigarettes were currency in prison. I stayed with Babs for a whole year when I went to London to do Speech Therapy.

Years before in 1956, with money from Aunt Kitty; through Babs MA borrowed the Scottish Woman's Alpine Club's chalet in St Luc, Switzerland for a month, we also stayed at Chateaula School at Montreux. We had a wonderful holiday.

Babs used to come to stay with us in Woodford regularly and one weekend MA took her sailing with the Seivewrights, friends who had a boat. She loved it and caught the sun and went back to London bronzed. She was talking to the parents of the children in her school play when they mentioned how well she looked. "Oh I've been sailing", she said, "I want to get a boat!"

"We have a boat the children have grown out of and never use, we will send it round to you!" said Mr and Mrs Sacker (M & S)! So Babs came into my room at her house in Finchley and said, "Would you like a boat?" It was a 'Lymington Scow' delivered that summer to Christchurch sailing club. It was called 'Rock n Roll', a really wonderful little gunter-rigged dingy that would hold 4 adults and a case of beer, and go out in a force 4 gale very happily. I later kept it at Pool Harbour Yacht Club where there was a long jetty. I had to varnish it every year, it was clinker–built and had to be sunk each year to swell the timbers. Babs came to stay with me in Mauritius when Jonathan was in London borrowing her house. She came to Reunion Island with our climbing club. He said to me when he got back to Mauritius, "Stop missing Babs!" She was very good company. She was a wonderful conversationalist full of anecdotes.

Babs remained a very good friend always, unfortunately M A killed her in a car crash!

She had come to stay to recuperate after a broken hip, and after the car crash she broke her pelvis and never really recovered.

She left me her ormolu desk which had spent the war in Jenner's cellar in Edinburgh, I believe and also the corner cabinet. She rang me up before she died and told me she wanted me to have them.

She was rich and had a stockbroker brother who was very rich, she told the story of him and his wife who had been to the Ideal Home Exhibition and in bed that night the wife confessed to him, "I bought a very, very expensive mink coat," he rolled over and said to her, "I bought a Rolls Royce!"

Babs was very generous and very lonely. She bought friends. She had a nice house in Kingston and promised her neighbours that she would leave it to them in her Will.

(She had said to George that she would buy Mr. Parker's house and leave it to him), this was a natural reaction, when she was staying with my mother and the house next door was for sale, they were old friends, but of course it did not happen.

Her neighbours took her seriously, when they moved down to Lymington, they built a granny flat for Babs and she was put in it. She hated it and would ring up my mother to complain. She died there after the car crash.

Others

Another friend was POOR Joyce. Also ex India, her husband Archie was very fat. He would roll on her at night. He gave her a fur coat and an Alsation dog attacked her! There was always a sad story!

Mrs Heath came to stay, she was known as 'the cobra' she stayed for nearly a year. She was very mean and when she left she gave Mrs Feltham an old glasses case, Mrs Feltham said, 'I don't wear glasses!', Mrs Heath said, 'One day you might!'

Mrs Feltham was MA's best friend. They had breakfast together and a mid-day drink together and talked and laughed together. She just loved Mrs F!

There were so many friends who over the years all said, 'Oh Mary Ann do you remember IN INDIA?, IN INDIA ! It would ring through the little cottage.

GENERAL PHOTOGRAPHS, PESHAWAR 1930S

Eddie hiring ponies with his dog in camp

Self, with Sherpas climbing

Ponies carrying our kit with Eddie

Sherpas on the snowfield

Self, climbing

Tackling the moraine

Picnicking in Gulmarg

Trekking

IN HER NINETIES

Loving life...

Muriel Lowis with Rosemary and Sarah in Gulmarg, 1941

Hoebridge where Rhona Rutherford was brought up

Appendix 1

DERIDRE LOOMBE'S LETTER OF CONDOLENCE

29th December 1992

Dear Sarah,

I was so sorry to read in your Christmas card about your mother's death. You must miss her very much. Last time I spoke to you she was in hospital but I hoped she would be all right. I used to so much enjoy coming up to see her at your flat and also during that lovely week-end we had in Suffolk. She was so interesting to be with and was always so incredibly alert and such FUN. You never felt any age barrier with her. She just seemed of our generation. So easy to talk to and so interested in other peoples lives. She was really amazing and such a spirited woman. You felt she had tremendous reserves of resilience and that life would never keep her down. I feel very glad to have known her even in a small way. She was such an individual and it was always so refreshing to meet someone who didn't follow the crowd and was very much her own person. I am sure there will be many people who will miss her very much.

So dear Sarah, much sympathy, Hope to see you early in the New Year.

Love from Deidre.

Appendix 2

HARRY'S LETTERS FROM THE FRONT 1915 -17

5.3.16

My dear Betty,

You seem to be having a busy time with your play and it must have been great fun getting it up and performing it so often. Sometimes London companies come over here to amuse the soldiers but we have not met any of them yet. However we have always plenty of work to keep us busy and the soldiers have not ceased to be entertained trying to speak to the French people. On the other hand they don't like them much because food etc is much dearer here than at home and Tommy always thinks they are cheating him.

We have been unlucky in coming to a miserable little village where the mud is awful and the sleeping accommodation very poor. Up at the front it is much better and quite a lot of my men are there just now getting instruction with another battery. In another week we shall take over a part of the line and support the infantry in the trenches and it is important that the men who will have to work the guns should see exactly what is expected of them in actual warfare.

How do you like the idea of going to live in Edinburgh? It will be a great change from Melrose and there will be lots of places to go and see and far more opportunities for amusements. Also after you have been to school you will make lots of new friends. I hope you will be pleased with the new house. In the holidays there will be Bamburgh to go to as usual and you always like being there.

We have had a lot of snow and frost lately but the snow never lies very long put prevents the ground drying up and the horses don't like the cold at all. They are not looking nearly as well as they did and I have had to send one or two to hospital. They must miss their comfortable stables and the straw they used to have to lie on.

With much love and many thanks for your nice letter,

Your own Daddy.

This is the last sheet of your xmas present.

29th July 1916

My dear Betty,

It was nice of you to cheer me up with a letter and I was awfully pleased to get it. Not of course that we are ever downhearted but in this noisy place it is pleasant to be reminded that you are all living peaceably and comfortably out of the war. I am glad you did well in your exams and are getting on well at St Georges. You will be quite ready for a holiday at the sea after all your exertions and there is no better spot than Bamburgh to spend it in. I should like very much to have a week with you there but under present conditions it is no use thinking about such things.

There is plenty for everyone to do here and as this is really the crucial time of the war we all want to be helping all we can.

You would be amused if you saw us popping out and into holes in the ground like rabbits, the Boche sent us lots of hate and we all spend our spare time digging deeper and deeper to get further away. Another advantage of a deep hole is that you don't hear so much of the guns. Some of the gunners are quite deaf with it and all of us are more or less so. None of us look the least like soldiers one sees at home. In this hot weather tunics are never worn but no one ever ventures out of his hole without a steel hat on just like a huge soup plate. Some of the men wear German and some French ones just as it suits their fancy, they vary both in shape and colour but they all turn bullets justly well.

This part of the country was occupied by Boche for quite a long time and there are all sorts of things lying about which they left behind. Letters and books are usually bought to me and sometimes these are very interesting and even touching. The Boche write nice frank letters and in nearly every one they hope that they will soon be peace. Very scarcely they say anything about hoping for victory and I dare say now they are not so hopeful about gaining it now. For we are pressing them very hard and they have got to leave one village after another. This is not at all nice for them as they have got to dig new trenches and make new fortresses to defend themselves while we occupy the ones they have just vacated and it is very hard work digging trenches

Well I cannot send you any particulars of what our troops are doing. You get all that in the newspapers before we do. All we are immediately interested in is a tiny wee bit of the front line a few miles long but it takes a lots of hard work to keep it in tact ready to push forward at any moment. With best love

Your own Daddy.

28.8.16

My dear Betty,

Many thanks for your nice long letter. I am glad you are having such a nice holiday and seeing some of your friends again. Even if all the old friends are not back in Edinburgh, it must be quite good sports getting to know new people.

We are back behind the range of German shells again and living in tents in the open but as the tents are always full of flies and it is too wet to go outside, life is not all pleasure. Fortunately they settle down at night so that we still get a little rest. It is quite strange at first to be able to walk across the fields and not have to creep along trenches or hide in shell holes. One soon gets used to anything.

Our present quarters are near a French aerodrome and we see the aeroplanes going and coming all day long. On the front the time to watch them is the afternoon when the light is good. At this time of day we had always 30 or 40 French or British planes over us and now and then a German fleet of 5 or 6 would appear approaching our lines. Immediately some of our men would dash to meet them and unless they were very quick in getting back there would be a fight high up in the air each side using machine guns. I have often watched these fights through glasses and admired the way the airmen guide their planes, twisting and turning about to avoid the bullets and get on to the enemy. It is daring work and generally ending one of the machines generally a Boche one falling headlong to the ground. We have better aeroplanes than the Germans and far more of them so they don't like fighting very much now. I can remember the time however when they were bold enough, but in this as in everything else they are getting beaten now. It is only a matter of time now until they will have to give in. I think another year will do it nicely and settle them for good. They will probably want to come to some arrangement with us sooner but we mustn't listen to them.

I am afraid this isn't a very interesting letter to write to a little girl but next time I shall try and think of something more pleasant. When you live in a country without any houses and nothing but soldiers and flies around you there isn't really much choice of subjects.

With best love your

Your own Daddy.

13.3.17

My dear Betty,

The letter you wrote me on 28th February only caught me up a day or two ago but I was glad to get your birthday good wishes and hear from you. My stay in Salisbury and London was fine and I enjoyed every bit of it although we were kept busy most of the day and I had to go off without any leave at the end.

I have now been back in the line long enough to get into the working of the battery on a new bit of the front and also to get used to the constant roar of the guns. Some bits of the German front line are more interesting than others because in some cases it is almost impossible to get a good view of it from the ground where I am, however there are lots of good places to observe from and it is more fun shooting when one sees where all the shells go. One also sees what the enemy are doing and can worry them quite a lot.

My new officers are all very young and are often very noisy, but they get on well together and work very well. At present we are building new gun pits and they are put to it to find the necessary materials as we can't get enough issued to us. This is a matter that requires more resource and imagination than fighting the Boches as purloining is severely 'verbotens' but we manage to get along and it is not the province of the Battery Commander to ask too many questions. We have got a comfortable mess at present but it is too far away from the guns to be quite handy so we are also digging another one beside them. The dining room is about 15 feet by 8 feet and the bedrooms are 6ft by 3 ft. all well underground and covered over with steel sheets and earth. This is the safest kind, but it does not lend itself to conventional ways of living. However with a good Cook and gramophone it is wonderful how well one gets along in a place of that kind. The A/63 (tank/cook) is by a long way the best of his kind that I have come across in France. Bully Beef forms the basis of our meal every day and so far he has not served it up the same way twice. But no potatoes now but he generally gets us a vegetable of some kind or other. We have at last got an excellent gramophone and about 200 good records including waltzes' and foxtrots to which the subs frequently dance after dinner.

The weather out here is quite spring like and mild now and life is getting quite pleasant although the mud hasn't quite disappeared. There is also far more shooting going on so one has to be careful, but it has not got really severe yet. Now and then one sees little pictures of houses going up in the air and occasionally there are barrages of shrapnel put on roads and trenches. .

I have had letter from Mummy from London but expect you are all back in Nelson Street Marion included and glad to get settled down as a family again. I have no doubt however that you enjoyed your stay with Viola at Royal Terrace and had a good time there.

With love to you all

Your own Daddy.

7.4.17

My dear Betty,

I got your letter all right and was very glad to hear from you again. I hope you had a good time during the holiday in spite of not getting to Bamburgh and will be able to put in the time you have still in hand. It was a pity to miss spending Easter at Bamburgh but the times are not exactly normal we are all put up with inconveniences.

Our underground dwelling is not too bad although there is not much room for us all and the entrance is rather dank and steep. It would be nice and cool in the summer time but this weather everything gets rather damp and muddy. We have had quite a lot of snow and rain these last few days and some of it finds its way inside through the ground. Sometimes a shell comes along and knocks down another house and makes a big hole in the ground but these don't worry us much.

There is an old friend of mine commanding a battery about 200 yards away and the other day I met a staff officer wandering along the battery position who came up to me when he saw me to ask the way to my friend's battery. It was the old adjutant of 159th Brigade and he nearly dropped when he recognised me. So we ran across one another. But as a rule we meet very few people except those with whom we are associated.

We are moving again and that is always a worry, one has to have at least double the amount of kit allowed by regulations, but when a Battery has to move the government does not supply sufficient transport to carry the extra kit and it takes a lot of scheming to get it all moved.

With love to you all and many happy returns of the day,

Your own Daddy

Harry Sanderson comes across as a very gentle, loving man.

Appendix 3

COLLECTED POEMS: JAMES ELROY FLECKER, MARTIN SECKER, MARY ANN'S SCRIBBLES

Poem 1931

By Marion Sanderson

Swallows

St Francis preached to swallows (long centuries pass bye)
In the woods of Assissi,
He thought he'd do them service
And show them how to die,
With a crude repentant tear drop
In each bright inquiring eye.

St Francis loved the swallows,
But he could not quite approve
Of their happy careless freedom,
Which he felt he must reprove,
That they might join the Saints above
In blameless rectitude.

Although we love the swallows
We don't preach to them today
We show our friendly feelings
In a very different way,
We take them near to Heaven
But they are not allowed to stay

Now a pilot drops the swallows
From his high powered aeroplane,
Among the gnats and insects
Of the rich Italian plain,

(Not a bad exchange for heaven
And easier to attain.)

P34

Poesy and cant, what is the recipe, does anyone know? Rhyme doesn't count
neither does magical nonsense and mystical flow, To Hell with it all!

P37

The world is beautiful varied grand
And youth is eager, but to grasp its joys
To view its wonders and to understand
Something of men and things
Yet happiness eludes the outstretched hand
Is here one moment, laughs then draws us sad.

P38

Oh for happiness that unrewarding content
Grasped for one unreflecting hour and gone again
Can never stay within the hearts of men

Lightning Source UK Ltd.
Milton Keynes UK
UKHW020809140219

337276UK00003B/12/P